Arise My Daughter

A Journey from Darkness to Light

By: Barbara Alpert

Unless otherwise identified, all scripture quotations are taken from the following. Scripture quotations marked NIV are taken from the HOLY BIBLE, NEW INTERNATIONAL VERSION ®. Copyright © 1973, 1978, 1984 by International Bible Society. Used by permission of Zondervan. All rights reserved. Scripture quotations marked TM are taken from *THE MESSAGE*. Copyright © 1993, 1994, 1995, 1996, 2000, 2001, 2002. Used by permission of NavPress Publishing Group.

Disclaimer: The author is not a licensed therapist or counselor. The enclosed information is strictly the experience and opinion of the author. If treatment or counsel is needed it is highly recommended that individuals seek a trained professional. See list of recourses, at back of book for professional assistance.

ISBN-13: 978-1484931011

ISBN-10: 1484931017

Praise for *Arise My Daughter*
A Journey from Darkness to Light

"Arise My Daughter" opens our eyes to "see" into the private world of people who appear to be all put together yet live in torment everyday. Barbara has given us a personal view of her private anguish. Thank God for His redeeming love, mercy, and grace! No matter what Satan tries to do to us "greater is He that is within us"! After reading *"Arise My Daughter"* I wanted to shout one word. VICTORY!"   —Toddy Jadoo

"Arise My Daughter" captured my uninterrupted attention from page one. I never lost focus and I did not put it down until finished. I found the questions at the end of each chapter to be very helpful; I realized I needed to answer those questions for myself. I wrote down so many thoughts that I became aware of through the author's words. The main message I received is that when it was just the author and God, she found serenity. I've learned to "Let Go and Let God" and in doing so, I have found my serenity. I know this book will be an inspiration to many." — Donna Morlock

"This is an amazing true story about a courageous Body Dysmorphic Disorder and suicide survivor coping through tragedy. As a suicide & BDD survivor myself, it was a must read for me, and impossible to put down. The author spoke on behalf of me too! Thanks for allowing my voice to be heard through your words. *"Arise My Daughter"* allowed me to become aware of some of my own bad feelings. I learned so much about my relationship with God and Jesus. I feel closer to the Lord now than ever before." —Tamara Bulhack

Praise for *Arise My Daughter*
A Journey from Darkness to Light

"Arise My Daughter" is an awe-inspiring read. It was written from a position of purity and humility flowing through the author's heart. Her journey will capture your attention, as God captures your heart. You will never be the same as God touches you through her. God bless you and empower you, as you embark on your own journey, from your own darkness to God's loving Light. What God does for one, He will do for another. Nothing is impossible for God to heal, renew, restore." —Deborah Varney

"Arise My Daughter" is a heart-rending narrative of Barbara's struggle with a mind-boggling disorder that kept her prisoner within herself for many years. Her courage and fortitude during her battle to stay alive and conquer her terrors is an inspiration that first broke my heart, and then made it sing with her triumph. This is a must-read for anyone who struggles with a psychological illness, and who deeply desires to be free. Thank you, Barbara, for your candor and honesty, and for teaching us the meaning of true spirit and trust in God. —Jean Archambault-White, Author, Simple Faith; Eloise of Westhaven (the series)

"The numerous graphic, detailed, horrific personal happenings and experiences, as well as the testament of the marvelous life changing miracle of Salvation, Deliverance, and Healing through JESUS CHRIST, were painstakingly written with deep conviction of forever imprinting the heart and mind of the readers. May God bless this endeavor." —Jo Ann Davis

Dedication

I dedicate this book to my two precious daughters, Christina and Stephine. I extend my utmost apology for not being the healthiest of moms. Unfortunately, the harsh, cruelties of this world held me captive to an inner prison of dismay, which touched your lives. However, through the love of Christ and determination to become well, I found the way out. Thank you both for loving me regardless of my flaws. I love you both dearly.

I wish to extend a huge "thank you" to my devoted husband, Dave. Thanks for putting up with my extreme highs and lows during this deep healing process. Thanks for depositing your unfailing love, peace, and security into my inner turmoil. It was part of the antidote of me becoming well. I always told you, "God's getting me better so I could be a blessing to you and others." I pray that the Lord continues to protect and bless our hearts and home, as we journey through this lifetime together and into eternity.

This book is also in memory of my youngest sister, Kim. My intentions were to share it with you in hopes that it would lead you to your own path of healing. However, you are no longer here and I can only hope and pray that it will be of great help to many other hurting women. May you rest in peace now that your "wild roller coaster" through life has ceased. I miss you dearly.

Special thanks to Dona Lee Gould for her editorial services and support. Sincerest thanks to everyone else in helping make this God given dream become a reality and worldwide ministry.

"I didn't die. I lived! And now I'm telling the world what God did." —Psalm 118:17 (The Message)

Preface

When an individual experiences multiple tragedies during ones early developmental years, how then is one to live a "so-called" normal life? Trauma, after trauma, after trauma, with no proper healing taking place, can cause even the strongest of minds to become dysfunctional, especially the formative mind of an innocent child. I only recall a few vivid memories of my early childhood. It is just enough to remember where I came from, why I ended up becoming the person I was, and who I am today.

For forty years, I rode a wild roller coaster I thought would never end. I believed I would not make it out alive, and death often looked better than life. With God and my determination to become well, the hellish ride slowly disintegrated and finally ended. Today, I am thankful to have survived the tragedies from my past and now look forward to living a blessed life of meaning and purpose. No more attempts to escape living, no more masks to be worn, just free to be the real me—a precious daughter of the Lord, who is finally able to receive and extend love unto others. Truly, there is a "Light" at the end of the tunnel…not just for me but for you, too!

I pray that my journey from darkness to the "Light" leads you to your own path of healing; setting you free to become the real woman God destined you to be! I hope that by you answering the questions at the end of each chapter and seeking God in prayer regarding your own inner battles, you will be on your way to healing, transformation, and freedom to live a more blessed life. As an extra bonus, make sure to read the all-inspiring, life changing *"Arise My Daughter"* message at the end of the book. It will surely bless you in going forward in life and your walk with the Lord.

Let the journey begin…

Contents

Chapter

"For I know the plans I have for you," declares the Lord, "plans to prosper you and not to harm you, plans to give you hope and a future."

—Jeremiah 29:11 (NIV)

One

Tragedy One & Two

While playing at the sandbox with my kindergarten classmates, I heard a deep, loud voice transmitting over the school's intercom system. When I heard my name on the loudspeaker, sand passed through my fingers as in an hourglass. Mrs. Shultz, my teacher, grasped hold of my hands and said, "Barbara, come now you have to go home." We walked to the coatroom where she helped with my coat. She turned me towards the doorway and standing there were my siblings. As we held hands, we walked down the hallway, sensing something bad. I do not recall if we even talked as we journeyed down that endless, cold, and eerie corridor toward the main office.

It seemed like a very slow, long walk to the end of the hall where our uncle was waiting for us. Remorsefully he said, "I have to take you all home." We left the building clutching each other's hand. My uncle stuffed us all into his car and headed for home. Till this day, I do not recall what went through my mind during the ride back. I just know it seemed to take a longtime to get home, as if he was driving deliberately slow.

Next thing I recall, I was leaning against my grandmother's old washing machine, distancing myself from the commotion in the house. An old-fashioned radio sat atop it. I heard a broadcast on the radio saying a man's body was found "dead." Somehow, I felt the dead man was my daddy. *Why is everyone crying? Where is mommy? Why are all these people here? Where are they all coming from?*

I have absolutely no idea what happened from that point on. I do not recall seeing Mom that entire day. Supposedly, I later heard that relatives had hidden her from us because she was devastated. After all, when Dad decided to take his life, by hanging, he left Mom, at age twenty-seven, a young widow with seven children: Debby, Danny, Sandy, Barbara (me), Michael, Jimmy, and Kim. We were all under the age of nine, and Kim was a mere four months old.

My mind must have blocked everything else out from the horrible event. *Did I cry? Did I attend my father's funeral? Did I receive counsel?* I do not remember experiencing one day with Dad. His suicide is the only thing I recall, envisioning him hanging from a tree. And from that day, there was a long span of walking through life, where I just existed and have little memory of anything but going to school and going home.

When I came out of my fog, it was to face the next vivid memory of childhood, an even greater tragedy. I have almost no remembrance whether or not the years, prior to this next tragic event, were good or bad. It seems as if someone went into my mind and deleted nearly every single detail. From the time I was five, until the time I reached eleven, is practically a blank slate.

There are blurs and cloudy memories of some things like hiding in cubbyholes in the attic of our three-story home with my dolls. I often sought to escape the nonstop commotion taking place throughout our house. I could not tolerate the blaring sound of numerous TVs, constant bickering of people, and the barking and howling from our four dogs. On top of searching for quietness in cubbyholes, I frequently experienced horrible nightmares. I recall waking up shaking & shivering, and crying at the top of my lungs. Often, my grandma allowed me to jump into her bed, so I didn't have to worry about the demons trying to kill me while I slept. I hated going to sleep because of those dreadful nightmares.

The next disastrous recollection erupts during the summer of 1975, when a fire destroyed our entire home. Nearly every possession we had owned was destroyed including the life of my stepfather, Scott. Mom remarried seven years after dad's death, yet I have very limited memory of him. He and Mom were married for only a few months before this shocking incident took his life. While trapped in this horrific event, I clearly see myself sitting on the roof of our three-story house, fully engulfed with flames. Thirty years later, I can still see, smell, and even feel the magnitude of the intense blaze, the stench of smoke, the fear of death, the chaos and horror that surrounded me, and besieged my family.

The fire that roared through our home started in the late evening hours while we slept. I was startled awake by Grandmother Rita's frantic shouts. Her voice scared me because she was shouting at the top of her lungs, "Get out! Get out! The house is on fire! Get out!" Yet she was nowhere to be found. Quickly, my two older sisters, Debby and Sandy, and I jumped out of our beds and ran into the adjoining bedroom where Mom and my younger sister were sleeping. When we ran into the room, I remember seeing flames, already burning through the bedroom windows. Even the very bed they lay sleeping in caught fire. Debby rushed to Mom's side and yelled for her to awake. Mom aroused from her bed and grabbed hold of my little sister. We all rushed back into the other bedroom.

Only one door, led out of the third floor attic, where we slept. The door led down to the second floor and out to safety. However, such was not the case that night. When Mom opened the door, the staircase filled with black, thick, smoke, and blazing flames stunned us. We continued to hear Grandma Rita yelling, "Get out! Get out! The house is on fire! Get out!" We were trapped! We couldn't go down the stairs. Mom slammed the door shut and quickly searched for another way out. She decided we ought to flee through a window that led onto a small roof. She pried it opened so we could use it for our escape. Petrified, I refused to go out and started to put up a struggle. I was frightened, hysterically wanted to try to make it down the stairs, even though I'd seen all the smoke and flames. Though my three sisters scrambled out the window, I still refused. Mom finally grabbed my hair and with all her might forced me out the window.

Outside, we huddled together on the tiniest piece of roof, and screamed for help. Flames shot up and out of the windows, whipping at the roof we sat on. Our eyes watered, we coughed, and choked, as the heavy smoke wrapped around us. My youngest sister, Kim, slid toward the edge of the roof and tumbled over the edge. Terror paralyzed me. We were over three stories up and a concrete walkway lay below, I feared Kim had died. Even with her gone, there was still not enough room for the four of us.

Over to my left, past Mom, I saw a firefighter take Debby down a ladder. Shortly after, another appeared and took Mom. Sandy and I held each other tightly, waiting for our rescue. Suddenly, the window behind us exploded. As the flames landed on my arms, I smacked embers off but everything I touched was hot. I started to slide down the inclined roof, trying to scurry back I kept scraping my bare legs on the rough sandpaper like roof. As soon as the firefighter returned, I leapt into his arms, leaving Sandy behind, to be the last.

When I reached the ground, I frantically searched for my great-grandmother, Mary. I cherished her beyond reckon. She meant the world to me and I could not imagine living life without her. Among all the chaos and confusion, I finally found her sitting under an old grapevine, far away in our backyard. Tears streamed down her face, which was etched with disbelief. I ran to her for comfort, not yet knowing the fate of the rest of my family.

After seeing that she was safe I searched for the rest of my family, and came upon firefighters working on Sandy. The firefighters poured water over her arms and legs as she lay on the ground, charred. I watched, recoiling from the terrible odor of burnt flesh. She kept repeating strange words. The pain was causing hallucinations. Paramedics arrived and put her on a stretcher, and whisked her away. Suddenly, I heard a massive explosion and looked up to see more flames shooting out. As the drumming of the explosion ended, I heard the loudest scream I've ever heard in my entire life. I held my breath and listened until I realized– my stepfather was trapped inside. He died– as there was no way anyone could have survived that burning inferno.

> *"...When you walk through the fire, you will not be burned;*
> *the flames will not set you ablaze."* — Isaiah 43:2 (NIV)

As the blaze continued to mount, I edged toward the front of the house, carefully, to keep away from the burning flames and falling embers raining down upon the scene. I could not believe my eyes. "Wow" was all I could utter as I witnessed my entire home engulfed in a rage of fire. When you find yourself in the middle of a major catastrophe, it seems there are no words to express the terrifying experience. Fire trucks, hoses, ambulances, flashing lights, screams, fumes, tears, are all mingled together in my mind.

Finally, a neighbor took my hand and led me to an ambulance. I was placed inside and given oxygen. Some of my siblings were already inside and I was the last they could fit. The paramedics shut the doors and sped us to the hospital.

I was wheeled into a hospital room with one of my siblings. The nurses told me to keep breathing deeply as a machine helped rid my lungs of smoke. They told us Mom was all right but, because she was pregnant, they had her in ICU. After several breathing treatments, the nurses tried to wash me up because my entire body and hair was covered with black soot and smoke. They tried wiping me down with soap and water, while I remained in bed. However, the water and towels kept turning black after a mere few wipes. Frustrated at the lack of progress, they finally resorted to a shower. I watched the black water pour off my body making its way toward the drain. They washed me repeatedly and the water turned grey, and then lighter grey, but even after multiple showers, I still reeked of smoke.

My memory of the time after the fire is severed. I don't recall a funeral, or even being told of my stepfather's death. I don't know if I even cried. My three brothers made it out of the fire with only minor injuries along with Debby and I. Kim remained in the hospital in critical condition for a long time. Sandy, burnt on both arms and legs suffered through years of skin grafts and physical therapy, but luckily, they both survived. Mom was physically all right and four months later gave birth to her eighth and final child, Scott.

Immediately after the fire, the entire community came to our rescue. They collected money, donated clothing, food, and provided immediate shelter for our entire family. Thank goodness for their generosity. It helped us out tremendously for without it, we would surely have been lost. We would have never made it if it were not for their kind hearts and support. We lost nearly everything in the fire except our lives and the inescapable nightmares that ensued.

Numerous newspapers declared our house fire to be the worst recorded in our hometown. However, good arose out of this tragedy. Shortly after the fire, a town ordnance was passed enforcing homes to install smoke detectors. For two months, the local fire departments handed out free smoke detectors to anyone in need. In addition, many firefighters were injured on the scene while battling the blaze. In an effort to prevent further firefighter injuries the local fire departments decided to use video coverage of the fire for training purposes.

Father God, Although I did not know You in my early years, I thank You for being with me through those horrible events that took place. Thank You for walking through the fire with me and not allowing the flames to set me ablaze. Thank You for providing for my family in our time of great need through the gracious support of a caring community. Amen

- Have you ever experienced any early childhood trauma?
- If so, did you receive proper counseling in dealing with such distress?
- Could you still be "inwardly" struggling with some of those issues today?

I continued to gorge on food to soothe my inner pain. I didn't know any other way to escape from the torment within and around me. Unfortunately, this habitual routine led me into obesity. By the time, I entered the sixth grade I weighed a whopping 170lbs. I hated going to school. Yet I had to, regardless of how dreadful I felt about my gruesome size. Everyone in my elementary school knew what happened to my family over the summer. The fire that destroyed our home and killed my stepfather was the worst fire ever recorded in our hometown. I believe the teachers, as well as my classmates, were sympathetic towards my obese condition. However, attending school with no one knowing what to say to ease my pain caused me to sink into an ever-deepening spiral of despair.

By the time my sixth grade graduation approached, I topped the scale at 180lbs. I became hysterical when school officials stated all the girls had to wear dresses for graduation. Within my wretched mind, this shocking news was worse than anything else I had experienced. The thought of finding a large enough dress to fit my enormous body was unimaginable. I cried hysterically when I got home from school, trying to explain the horrible situation to Mom. Talk about an emotional break down. Mom finally realized my weight had become a huge problem. She suggested I join Weight Watchers, but it was far too late. Graduation day was a mere two weeks away.

By chance, I found a dress big enough to fit my fat body, but it was not a pretty sight. I felt like a huge elephant, out of place, standing with the other students. An ugly, bright yellow dress, with hideous white eyelet fringes around the arms, repulsively draped my bulging body. While walking down the aisle to receive my diploma my dress repeatedly stuck between my chafing thighs. With every other step I took, I yanked the culprit out. With each pull, my face became warmer and warmer while everybody watched. I knew some of them laughed at me, pointing their fingers my way. The indescribable shame and humiliation I felt that day, caused me to turn to food even more. As a result, I grew bigger and bigger over the summer months. All too soon, it was time to make the transition into middle school and I was ill-fitted to handle the transgressions lurking ahead.

I never realized how cruel teenagers could be until I entered middle school. The new students laughed and teased me about my size. It was downright awful–the pain, humiliation, and grief they inflicted upon me. My appalling size finally caught up with me and I was paying for it now. The terrible things the students put me through were down right humiliating.

Not a single day went by without incurring some form of embarrassment or abuse at school. I dreaded going to my locker each day. The students habitually stuck mounds of chewing gum all over my lock making it difficult to get open. Numerous times, I found myself having to seek the janitor and ask, "Could you please come and remove the gum from my locker?" Often, the students stood around laughing while I waited to get into my locker. I felt singled-out for this never-ending torture. With the locker situation out of hand, I carried the majority of my books. Unfortunately, the bullies didn't like this idea. As a result, they often pushed me down to the floor, causing my books to go flying everywhere.

Life worsened with every passing offense. I never felt comfortable going to Mom for help. I felt sad for her because she was battling a never-ending war with my rebellious and out-of-control siblings. I never thought to ask my sister, Sandy, for help because it was often her peers who tormented me. I started hating her with a profound vengeance. She was very slim and extremely attractive. Undeniably, I was the dead opposite. Jealousy and envy mounted up inside of me towards her. Having these deadly emotions stacking up inside was pure hell. Already filled with low self-esteem and placing hatred on top, made me a virtual time bomb. I have no recollection of graduating from middle school. I guess my mind still protects me in its own crafty way.

The transition into high school was similar to middle school. Yet, it was worse because of the anger and hatred trapped inside of me. Again, Sandy, a grade up, was the center of attention. I hoped to see the student body more mature by this time. However, such was not the case, and the grief and humiliation continued.

One afternoon, while having lunch in the cafeteria, students threw food at me. Heaps of food kept hitting me from every direction. By the time, I stood to yell "STOP!" food already dripped down my face and body. They did not have the decency to stop. Instead, they preceded laughing wildly while still flinging food my way. I couldn't hold back the tears. They poured down my face, as quickly as the spaghetti and chocolate pudding did. As I tried to remove the food from my hair and clothing, I turned around and caught a glimpse of my sister outside in the courtyard having a joyful time with her friends. The smile engraved upon her face while hanging out with them added to the hatred I had brewing towards her. I left the cafeteria crying, searching for the nearest exit. Thank goodness, one was near, for I couldn't exit fast enough. As I walked home, tears, anger, disgust inundated my mind and body. *I hate everyone. I want to kill them. Maybe if I lose weight they will like me.*

Talk about a dysfunctional life. Sad to say, by this time alcohol, drugs, and immoral sex invaded every area of my so-called home. The amount of anger and jealously I felt toward my sister, Sandy, became obvious as I acted on my toxic emotions. Often, I beat her severely out of sheer jealousy. I was being abused, and in return turned into an abuser as well. I was disgusted with myself because I desired to be and look like her. In hindsight, I was rejecting myself. Another reason I knew I had to take control of my life and shift it into a positive direction. *How can I turn my life around?*

I started my first diet at the age of fifteen while still in my first year of high school. I was determined to lose weight in an effort to prevent additional adversity. I believed losing weight would boost my self-esteem and earn acceptance from others. I stumbled across the popular Scarsdale diet and followed it faithfully, along with daily exercise. Remarkably, my weight went down quickly and my self-esteem improved. All perfect timing as I finally reached the age I could work. Working brought me additional self-esteem and respect; I now earned my own money. I took on numerous part-time jobs, buying my own healthy diet foods, beauty aids, and clothing.

Mom never had enough money to buy anything above the basics. Her Social Security checks never covered all the necessary expenses. Our household's needs outweighed her income and thus caused a great deal of stress on everyone. I resorted to hiding most of the items I desired to have and bought with my own money. It was terrible to have to live this way, but when one is in survival mode, you find ways to carry on. Trying to get one clean, dry towel on a daily basis for showering was hard enough. The other stuff—shampoo, soap, toothpaste—was considered a bonus whenever around. I hated when Mom would tell me to let my siblings use the toiletries I had bought and put away for myself. In my mind, this was not fair, but grudgingly I did it anyway.

Losing more and more weight, I started to receive compliments. It made me feel good about myself for a change. As a result, I became more strong-minded, staying on track with my diet and exercise routine. I fully enjoyed walking to my various jobs, knowing it contributed to additional exercise, and provided a means to escape being at home. I saved as much money as I could in order to buy my first car. I was thrilled when I became old enough to get my driver's license and bought my car shortly after. I was proud in accomplishing this goal on my own, because Mom never encouraged us in this manner. Becoming more independent and escaping for a few more hours from the insanity plaguing my family, I started to enjoy life a little bit more.

Unfortunately, my second and third year of high school I succumbed to spending my time partying. Instead of self-medicating on food, I now turned to drinking. No longer soothing the inner pain with food, alcohol became my new best friend. Neither helped, yet when drinking I became more social and ended up dating.

I became pregnant at the age of seventeen, while in my fourth year of high school. I was not excited about being with child at such an early age. Nevertheless, the news was no shock to my family. I was following the same path as my other siblings. Not only was I pregnant, but I was in a very abusive, controlling relationship as well. John took total control of my life, forcing me to quit work and school as well. He refused to allow me to go out in public because he didn't want any other men looking at me. Not having any idea what a healthy relationship was like and longing for love, I accepted such mistreatment out of pure ignorance.

When I became aware of my pregnancy, I immediately quit drinking. I didn't want to bring harm to my unborn child. I took good care of myself during the entire pregnancy. Amazingly, I felt healthy and even pretty while pregnant. Unfortunately, John didn't agree. He continuously ridiculed me over the way I looked. He told me I was getting fat and I had better lose the weight once the baby was born. Yet, according to the doctors, I gained the appropriate weight expected for any normal pregnancy. Dealing with his verbal abuse was difficult, coping with his alcohol misuse even harder.

Whenever he drank, which was almost daily, he became very violent and beat me for no apparent reason. Having been raised in a violent household, I didn't know this kind of mistreatment was not normal. One night, he punched me, and gave me a fat, bloody lip. The following day Mom asked what happened, and I finally told her about the abuse. My big brother learned of the abuse and beat the living daylights out of John. After the brutal confrontation, John swore he would never lay a hand on me again. I stayed at Mom's house during my pregnancy and John moved in with us. Mom allowed us to convert the attached back porch into an extra bedroom. We arranged to stay there until the baby was born and saved enough money for our own apartment. During the remainder of my pregnancy, John refrained from hitting me, but the verbal abuse continued. I was too naive to understand. Abuse is abuse, no matter what form it takes. In hindsight, the verbal and mental abuses were actually more harmful than the physical abuse. I believe we heal faster from physical wounds than those imbedded within our minds, hearts, and souls.

Father God, Pardon me for my ignorance in turning to substances for comfort instead of seeking You. As You know, Lord, back then I had no knowledge of You. God, as You have forgiven me of my transgressions, I too forgive those who have wronged me. Amen

- Have you ever been physically, mentally, or sexually abused?
- If so, did you turn to outside substances such as food, alcohol, or drugs to soothe your inner pain?
- If yes, are you still possibly using this same coping technique today?

"Teach me how to live to please you, because you're my God. Lead me by your blessed Spirit into cleared and level pastureland."

—*Psalm 143:10 (TM)*

Three

Arrival of My Precious Gift

I remember so clearly the day I went into labor. Excruciating pain pierced its way through my lower back while standing in Mom's living room.

Looking as if I had just seen a ghost, I cried out to my sister, Debby. "Something is wrong!" I expressed to her about the pain transcending through my back.

"Barbie, you are going into labor."

I looked at her with fear in my eyes, "The pain is horrible. I can't take it anymore!" She decided to take me to the hospital. As soon as we arrived, they hurried me into an examining room and before I knew it, my water broke. They rushed me into the delivery room; the baby was on its way. Debby accompanied me into the delivery room because I was terrified. She was a few years older than I was and already had a child of her own. This gave me a bit of comfort knowing she had already been through what I was about to experience. No sooner did they prop me into the birthing chair the baby's head emerged. Actually, the doctor and nurses were not ready, but the baby was.

They kept yelling, "Don't push! Don't push!"

I yelled back, "I'm not pushing. It's coming out on its own!" The nurses did their best to hold the baby in place until the doctor finished being prepped. Sure enough, as soon as they removed their hands, the baby popped out. Debby stayed right by my side during the entire delivery. I must say, I am thankful she accompanied me instead of John, the baby's father. Truth be told, I didn't want him to be around for the delivery, as I feared his company. I call it a blessing in disguise. I gave birth to a beautiful, healthy, little girl and named her Christina.

I enjoyed my newfound role of motherhood, in spite of the fact I was only approaching my eighteenth birthday. Knowing how to care for her came naturally. The love I had to offer Christina was unbelievable. I never realized the depth of love within me. This precious gift brought a new sense of meaning into my life. I determined, with all of my heart, to protect this child from all harm and cruelty. I couldn't imagine her having to go through the slightest of horrors that I had suffered.

A few months after Christina's birth, John and I decided it was time for us to get our own apartment. The back porch we previously converted into a bedroom was a bit cramped now with the addition of the baby. It had no heat and with the cold, winter months approaching, it was time for us to move on. What I thought was a good idea, turned into a living nightmare.

When we moved into our own place, the beatings quickly emerged again. I thought living in Mom's house was bad, yet this was definitely the worst of the worst. Everyday I feared for my life. When John came home from work and saw a bit of makeup on my face, he became enraged, shouting, swearing, and accusing me of cheating on him. Yet never once had I. He demanded that I go into the bathroom and remove the makeup. As I followed his command, he'd hover over me to make sure I obeyed his orders. Thank goodness, Christina wasn't old enough to understand what was taking place. My heart would have been crushed if she were harmed by the abuse I suffered. Often, I put Christina into her crib and closed the bedroom door so she would not get hurt.

I hated making dinner for John. He was impossible to please. It made me sick to my stomach the kinds of food he ate. John moved to the United States from Portugal and only liked the food he was accustomed to eating. Every Sunday we drove to the specialty food store to buy his cuisine. Our apartment stunk horribly each time I cooked his so-called real food. It didn't look real to me—the dried-out, cardboard-looking fish he bought. The darn thing had to soak in water over night in order to be cooked the following day. Every morning I got up to pack John's breakfast and lunch before he went to work. I was a bundle of nerves whenever I packed his lunch cooler. Packing each single item in precise order was mandatory. If I made an error, or if something were left out, he'd come home and strike me because of the mistake, shouting I was nothing but a disgrace to him. He accused me of deliberately leaving things out of his lunch cooler or putting them in the wrong sequence in order to embarrass him in front of his coworkers.

I never ate the food that John chose to eat. Having to cook two different meals all the time was a nuisance. He prohibited Christina and me from sitting down and eating with him. He always made us wait until he finished eating his meals. Then he allowed us to sit down and eat ours. I hated when John complained about how high the grocery bill was each week, as if it was my fault. Numerous times, I tried to tell him how much his specialty foods cost but he didn't want to hear it. He'd pounce on me even more whenever I tried to speak up, so I learned to silence myself.

During the cold winter months, John insisted on going to the bar to play cards with his friends. He demanded Christina and I go with him. However, he commanded us to remain in the car while he went in. He wouldn't leave the keys so I could put the heater on in hopes to keep Christina warm.

I would plead with John, but he would sternly say, "No! You'll be fine till I get back." Warning me, "You better not even think about getting out of this car to leave!" He assured me if I did, he'd hunt me down and kill both the baby and I.

As hours passed by and the car turned colder and colder, I cradled Christina in my arms, holding her close to my chest in an attempt to keep her warm. I was always frightened while waiting for John. The city streets where infested with street junkies who'd come up to the car windows asking for money. Then I'd have to deal with his drunkenness and belligerent words causing another chilling scene for the evening. How naive I was, allowing such abuse to continue. However, I was only eighteen years old and did not know how to escape from the living nightmare. How could I leave when I knew, without a doubt, he would kill us if I tried to escape from his sinister hands?

Finally, one day when the beating and abuse got out of hand, I realized I had to escape. My life, as well as my daughter's, was in jeopardy. John came home drunk from an afternoon outing and didn't like the fact that I was playing outside in the backyard with Christina. When I saw the malicious look on his face as he screamed at me to get into the house, I knew trouble was brewing. However, I didn't know I was about to lose my life.

As soon as Christina and I entered the house, John started cussing at me. I quickly put Christina into her crib so she wouldn't be in the middle of the quarrel. Sure enough, as soon as I placed her in he took a swing, hitting my eye and then my mouth. He continued to punch me. My eyes and lips swelled up almost instantly as John hammered away at my face. To make matters worse, each time I tried to fight back he'd wrap his hands around my neck, choking me till near unconsciousness. I heard Christina crying in the background and feared for her safety as he continued to beat me. I yelled, I screamed, I kicked, but none of it mattered. Completely enraged and out of control, he kept yelling he was going to kill me if I didn't stop screaming for help. The situation worsened and I continued to yell for help, hoping one of the neighbors would hear my plea. He desperately wanted to quiet me and forcefully held a pillow over my face, stifling my screams until I couldn't breathe anymore. I grew weaker and weaker as I continued to struggle. Air became scarce as John unrelentingly tried to suffocate me to death. Before losing consciousness, I pretended I was no longer breathing in hopes he would stop. I laid there motionless, lifeless, as I played dead. When he removed the pillow, he shook me a bit to see if I was alive, but I continued to fake my death hoping, the deadly attack would end. Unbelievably, it worked as John rose off me and walked into the other room as if nothing happened.

Right away, I aroused from my make-believe pose. I rushed out of the room hoping to grab a hammer from the hallway closet. I knew I needed some form of protection and the hammer was the closest thing I could get my hands on. Unfortunately, as soon as John realized I was still alive he rushed towards me again. He noticed the hammer in my hand and tried fiercely to take it away. At that point, I have no idea what came over me. The amount of strength and energy raging from within me was immense as I fought back. I suppose I was in survival mode, undoubtedly fighting for my life. It seemed as though all the pent-up rage and anger stored up inside of me finally erupted. The walking time bomb I mentioned in the preceding chapter exploded. I couldn't refrain from swinging the hammer at John as I shouted for him to leave me alone.

The situation worsened when John ran into the bedroom grabbing his gun. Pointing it directly at me, he insisted I put the hammer down or he'd shoot me. "If you try to leave with Christina, I will kill the both of you." There was no doubt in my mind he was going to shoot me, no matter what I did. Holding the gun so close to my head, I watched John's finger slightly tug back on the trigger. I was scared out of my mind and knew I desperately needed to escape. With all my might, I whacked John's head with the hammer. As a result, his gun dropped to the floor. Quickly, I ran to the phone and dialed 911. However, before I could speak a word, John tore the phone off the wall, disconnecting me from any help. At this pivotal point, I had no alternatives left except to tell him what he wanted to hear. I made a false promise, letting him know I would never leave. I bargained for my life and Christina's as well.

"I won't leave. I'm sorry. I won't go outside again." He accepted my lies and calmed down.

I heard Christina crying in her crib. "I need to go and take care of the baby."

He simply moaned, "Go ahead. And clean up your face while you're at it." He gestured this because I had blood on my face and bruises that needed tending.

Fortunately, he decided to walk down the street to buy some more beer. Thank goodness for this, because it permitted me the opportunity to get some urgent help. The phone John pulled from the wall no longer worked. For that reason, I went searching for the extra phone I had stored away. As I searched for the phone, I kept encouraging Christina to stop crying. Assuring her everything was going to be ok. I told her, "Mommy is gonna get us out of here." My heart went out to her because she was only a year old and had no clue as to what was taking place. Finally, I found the extra phone and frantically plugged it into the wall jack hoping for a dial tone. A sigh of relief escaped me as soon as I heard the sound.

I phoned Mom. "John tried to kill me and you need to come and get me right away!" I briefly told her the danger I was in and she assured me she would be on her way. I knew we were still not safe as we waited for Mom to arrive. I called 911 and asked them to send the police. I anxiously went through the apartment grabbing hold of several items I knew I would need for Christina. I didn't intend to ever step back into the place once I escaped. When I saw Mom's car pull up, I felt a sigh of relief.

"We need to get out quickly before he gets back," I shouted. I knew now this was going to be it—my great escape from the living nightmare. I grabbed Christina, the few things I collected, and ran to Mom's car. Never once did I look back. Never again did I consider trying to make this abusive relationship work. What my daughter and I went through that day pushed me over the edge and into the realm of reality. *I do not deserve this mistreatment. I am a loving and caring person. He will never change.*

I moved back into Mom's house. I was only nineteen, felt as though I had been through hell, and back a hundred-fold. Moreover, I had nowhere else to go. Immediately, I went back to work in order to care for Christina and myself. I did not want to be dependent upon John or Mom for anything. My determination gave me strength and ability to press on. John tried to stay in the picture, desiring visitation rights, but as time passed the desire faded away. I feared for Christina being in his presence and was relieved when he no longer pressed to see her. John was a major abuser and I needed to protect her from harm.

"God's a safe-house for the battered, a sanctuary during bad times."
—Psalm 9:9 (TM)

Why I stayed in this abusive relationship for nearly two years? I did not know any different. Growing up, surround by violence and abuse, I was ignorant to a healthy, normal way of life.

Dear God, Although I was veiled to Your love reaching out to aid me, I can see clearly now Your wonderful hands at work in my life. Thank You for sending my mom to rescue my daughter and me from harm. Thank You for my precious daughter, Christina, whom is still the apple of my eye no matter how old she might be. May You keep me as the apple of your eye, too! Amen

- Are you currently trapped in a bad relationship and feel as though you have no means of escape?
- If so, have you ever thought about contacting a domestic violence organization for insight and help?
- Are you aware that God desires to rescue you from those that assail you?

Four

More Misfortune

Living back at Mom's house, I began to date again. I met a young man who entered the bakery where I worked. After several months of conversations, he finally asked me out. He was extremely nice, however, I felt out of place in his presence. *I don't think I am the proper girl for him. He's fine, but I'm messed up.* When out on dates, he opened the car door, pulled my chair out when we sat to eat, and always spoke kindly. I never experienced good manners like this and his respectful attributes made me feel uneasy. It was weird, strange–having such a decent person in my life. My tarnished self-worth guided me to think this way. The abuse from my past made me feel as if I was damaged goods. Sad to say, I ended the relationship because I could not accept his kindness.

Shortly after, I met another person, at the same workplace, who acted sly and subtle. At first, I didn't understand what was taking place, but as time went on, I realized he was flirting. He was an older, married man who, I presume, wanted me.

One day he asked, "Barbara, could you baby-sit for me and my wife? I want to take her out on a date and we need someone to watch the kids."

I, being naïve, agreed. "Sure! Why not? I'll come over and baby-sit for you." Afterward he walked me out to my car, paid for my services, and followed it up with an unexpected kiss, right in front of his house! I didn't know what to make of the situation and left.

The following day he entered my workplace, "I like you a lot. I'm planning to leave my wife. May I take you out?"

I still don't understand why, but I agreed. How dumb of me to fall into such a trap. I became his bait, his playmate. We dated a few months and what a big mistake it was. I believed he meant to leave his wife. I was young and vulnerable. He was much older and cunning. Deep within I felt uneasy about the relationship. I didn't like the fact that he was sneaking around on his wife while seeing me. As I grew more uncomfortable with the relationship, I ended it finally. I realized he was not going to leave his wife. He was only using me. I felt ashamed for falling into such a bad trap. I felt even more tainted. I felt like dirty laundry and berated myself for another bad choice.

Pulling away from the dating scene seemed the most logical thing to do. I didn't want to deal with men anymore. I felt like a filthy, used rag. However, no amount of washing cleaned the disgusting residue trapped within. Guilt, shame, and nauseating feelings of being violated overwhelmed me.

I determined to do my best raising Christina, while still living at Mom's house. I found a better job and moved into a higher, respectable, office position. Work became my focus along with desiring better for my daughter. I wanted to save enough money to move out of Mom's. I wanted more for Christina and me. It was hard leaving her at Mom's while I went to work. The ruckus in the house often was unbearable, but I knew I needed to work and I had no one else to watch her. I would anxiously drive home wondering if she had survived the day. I carried around a great deal of guilt and shame, because I had no choice but to leave her in the same calamity I'd grown up in. I swore when she was born I would protect her from such, yet here I was falling back on my promise.

As time went on, I thought I was healed from my past relationships, and reconsidered dating. Christina approached three when I started to date once more. Out for the night, my sister introduced me to a man named Robert. He was polite, matured, and not abusive. Right away, our affection toward one another blossomed. What enhanced the relationship was the fact he did not mind that I had a young child. We enjoyed doing things together, going out, having fun. As I spent more time over his place than at Mom's, we decided it was time for us to get our own place. We found the perfect rental home, suitable for all three of us. It was a very nice place, something that was then unfamiliar to me. For the first time ever, I felt like a princess, my fairytale coming true. We made it our home and I began to live life in what I considered a better way. He worked, I worked, and Christina lived in a healthier environment. We had a nice life going.

Then one day, taken by surprise, I found out that I was pregnant, again. Being so young, only twenty-one, and unmarried tossed me into utter confusion. *What should I do? Will Rob marry me?* After discussing all our options, both Rob and I decided to wed. We had a simple, backyard wedding at my sister's house.

Undoubtedly, I was pleased with the decisions Rob and I had made. I became a wife and a wedded mother too. A few months later, I gave birth to another beautiful, little girl. We named her Stephine. Life was going well as we planned for our future.

While I gave birth to my second daughter, my great-grandmother Mary was also in the same hospital recovering from an illness. I floated in a realm of bliss, while being wheeled down to her room holding Stephine in my arms. I was filled with joy. How delightful it was to see my great-grandma holding my newborn child during our visit. I didn't want to leave her bedside, but I knew I had to go back to my own hospital room to feed Stephine. I promised Gramma I would be back to visit her once I recuperated at home from the delivery.

Shortly after our get-together, her health took a turn for the worse. *She waited for me to have the baby. She hung in there just for our visit.* As a result, a new nightmare was unleashed, and I became captive to the heartbreaking, tear-jerking circumstances. Witnessing her declining condition tugged at my heartstrings. Sad to say, I chose not to visit her anymore. It was too painful to see her fading away. I'd leave her hospital room feeling as though a part of me was fading along with her. Going home and tending to my newborn child felt weird. I felt numb, no emotions, no feelings, no pleasure. Something strange was taking place deep within my core. Struggling with death and life simultaneously, the pending death of my great-grandmother Mary and the recent birth of my daughter, Stephine baffled me, confusing my mind and emotions. Rob realized the struggle I was in and did his best to help.

My family frowned on my decision to pull back from visiting my great-grandma, but I had to do what was necessary for my survival. They didn't realize how deeply I cherished this woman. She meant the world to me. *She's dying. I'll never see her again.* When I heard the shocking news of her death, three months after the birth of Stephine, my entire body, heart, and mind deadened. My life suddenly froze, shattering my heart into pieces. My heartstrings tore as my heart broke, leaving me feeling hopeless. Grey–everything became grey. Life lost all color.

Attending her funeral service was excruciating, tremendously disturbing. Thank goodness, Rob accompanied me. Lifting myself out of the car was dreadfully painful. As I walked unsteadily towards the church, Rob stationed himself by my side, propping me up as though he was carrying me in. When we entered the church, everyone was sitting in the front pews. I sat in the very last one, trying to distance myself from her death.

Upon seeing her casket, I lost all composure, weeping and trembling hysterically. Rob, left with no choice, escorted me out of the church before the service ended. The tears, grief, and sorrow overwhelmed me. This was an intensity of heartache and mourning I never experienced before. Even though I experienced my father and stepfather's deaths, I do not believe I was old enough to comprehend the devastating loss.

The drive to the cemetery felt like my own death sentence. A huge part of me was buried alongside her that day. I chose to stay far away from the burial sight where everyone gathered, distancing myself from the rituals of her death. A dark cloud surrounded me, as though the light of day no longer existed. No rain needed to fall, for my tears flooded the day. When the service ended, we gathered at my sister's house. Ill at ease, I only stayed a short time. In my grief-stricken mind, I thought they were heartless gathering for food and drinks. *How could they eat and drink at a time like this? Is this what people do when someone dies? Where do the dead go? What is heaven?* My soul cried for Grandma Mary to hold me again, to shelter me from this pain, this emptiness. Upon leaving, unfathomable sorrow, sadness, and grief escorted me.

"You have taken from me my closest friends and have made me repulsive to them. I am confined and cannot escape; my eyes are dim with grief." —Psalm 88:8-9 (NIV)

A few days after her death, my tears ceased. My broken heart no longer wept, as though it was placed in its own casket. At this pivotal point, life became unbearable. My life, my world, shattered into pieces. I could not allow myself to love anyone—husband, daughters, not even myself. I built a wall to protect myself from additional grief and heartache. *I cannot love others, because they will die! I cannot be attached, because they will be torn away! I will be crushed again!* My grandmother's death pushed me into a realm I cannot even begin to explain. I was alive, but it felt as though I was dead — no emotions, no feelings, no love. My role as a caring, functioning wife and mother felt like a heavy burden instead of joy. I became my worst enemy and my beloved ones suffered because of it. I detached from all life, reality, and truth. Had I crossed into the same realm that my mother did?

Dear God, Thank You for sending Rob into my life. He was a help in my deepest hour of grief. Thank You for choosing me to give birth to my daughter Stephine. I praise You for bringing my closest friend, Gramma Mary, home to be with You. May she take delight in Your presence. Amen

---

- Have you ever lost someone that was very close to your heart?
- If so, have you properly mourned the loss or perhaps still struggling with accepting it?
- Have you built a wall around your broken heart, not wanting to be hurt again?

"There is a time for everything, and a season for every activity under the heaven: a time to be born and a time to die, a time to plant and a time to uproot,"

—Ecclesiastes 3:1-2 (NIV)

Five

Disorders Emerge

Disgusted with the weight I had gained during pregnancy, I grew miserable with my looks. In my distorted mind, I carried a ton of extra weight. In reality, it was not so. I fell into a deep state of self-hatred. *I hate my looks! I am ugly! I am hideous!* I have no idea what was wrong with me. I did not know how to live or function anymore. I sought numerous ways to alter my so-called, repulsive appearance, but nothing worked. Changing the color of my hair from brown to blonde was a waste. In fact, it made things worse because my hair turned orange. Changing the color of my eyes from brown to violet didn't work either. The ugliness lingered within me, no matter what I did outwardly.

"When my heart was grieved and my spirit embittered, I was senseless and ignorant; I was a brute beast before you."
—Psalm 73:21-22 (NIV)

I took my gruesome anger out on my children. Yelling, screaming, and swearing at them because I hated myself, everything about myself. The unbearable rage within me grew and grew and I could not get it under control. For some reason, unknown to me, I pushed the blame onto my children. My mind convinced me that the rage and anger I battled was due to them. *What is wrong with me? This is not normal! Am I cursed?* I wonder if this cruel behavior was passed down to me. It was all so familiar while growing up.

Often, vindictively, I would bawl to my husband, "I can't handle the kids! I don't know how to be a mom to them! I would rather be dead! I'm a horrible mother!"

He would politely calm me down, "Barb, you don't really mean that. Things will get better."

I despised myself and my beloved ones took the brunt of it. I knew things were getting worse as I began to think morbid things about my children. The knowledge made me hate myself even more. It was eerie not knowing what had taken place in my heart and mind. At the time, I did not know I battled with a severe form of Post Partum Depression accompanied by several other psychological disorders.

Even though I tried to keep my composure with the children, the rage and anger still erupted each time I looked in the mirror. I entered a torture chamber every time I stepped into the bathroom to groom myself. I tried to change, but my irrational behavior continued to get worse. Rob and I thought maybe if we relocated, it might solve some of my problems. We bought a two-bedroom condominium on a private beach in high hopes that this would remedy my condition. However, such was not the case. The war with the bathroom mirror followed me wherever I went. My mind took a death-defying dive for the worse, an ever-increasing inner rejection and torment aimed at myself.

At first, I attempted to hide the inner turmoil I battled–the ugly, unattractive, warped image I carried. I did everything humanly possible to make my outside world look picture perfect. I obsessed, focusing on my looks, weight, home, and children. Everything had to be clean and neat at all times. I cringed each time the kids sat down on the sofa to watch television. I anxiously waited for them to get up so I could straighten out the cushions. It seemed as though I was walking on a bed of nails. Whenever they were playing with their toys in the living room, I immediately told them to clean it all up as soon as they finished. Often, I went through their bedroom discarding anything and everything that looked as if it was clutter.

Grocery shopping became another bizarre ritual. I refused to allow anyone to bag my food. I placed every item into the bags myself so they were in proper order. I hated going down any aisle that had mirrors or reflections, because they reminded me of the conflict I undertook at home—hour after hour grooming myself. Often, I panicked while shopping, a feeling of being smothered by everyone clouding my mind. Anxiety and panic overcame me when anyone passed by. Numerous times, I almost abandoned my cart, wanting desperately to escape from the feelings of paranoia. During these perturbed times, I quickly rushed through the rest of my shopping, dodging towards the exit as soon as I was done.

Living on the beach and being preoccupied with cleanliness was not easy. The girls wanted to go out to play and I obsessed over getting the sand off them. It was a joy for them, but it was torture for me. Hosing the girls down, vacuuming what little sand made its way in, all performed in an extreme compulsive manner. I wanted my daughters to enjoy things so I continued to do my best to hide my inner war. I didn't want to be a bad mom. I wanted to be a healthy mom.

I finally realized I needed professional help. I saw a doctor, who immediately put me on medication for anxiety. She told me to take the medication a half-hour before going into the bathroom. She diagnosed me with a condition called, OCD, Obsessive Compulsive Disorder. The medication helped slightly, but it didn't remove the ugly visions I saw reflected in the mirror. It only allowed me to stay calm.

The preoccupation with my looks took a toll on my family. Obsessed with my weight, I developed an eating disorder called Anorexia Nervosa. The paranoia with my weight cruelly controlled my life. I prohibited myself from most foods, in order to maintain control. The bathroom scale became my newest friend, or perhaps my worst enemy. Day in and day out, I weighed myself—morning, noon, and night, making certain I wasn't gaining any weight. Eventually, this was not good enough. I began to weigh myself nearly every hour. It felt as though I functioned under a spell, stepping on the scale more and more. As I ate less and less, my weight decreased more and more.

My exercise obsession took preference over caring for my children and husband. I could not tolerate anyone or anything until I exercised for the day. Even though I lost a great deal of weight, my mind convinced me I was getting fatter and fatter. I restricted my food intake and upped my exercise rituals to an unhealthy degree. My weight continued to drop, but every time I looked in the mirror, all I could see was this fat, ugly person starring back at me. On the contrary, I was so underweight, nearly every single bone in my body showed. I looked like a skeleton, a bag of bones. The insanity was so intense, yet I could not stop it. I hated my life more and more as another deadly disorder engulfed me.

I dreaded going to family get-togethers, holidays, and all special occasions. They interrupted my need to be in control over what I ate, when I ate it, and more importantly my exercise routine. Planning a family vacation was torture. The thought of having to groom myself in a hotel room around my husband and children terrorized me. I didn't want them to endure the outpourings of my obsessions and compulsions and the battle in front of the mirror, a war between two individuals who just didn't see eye to eye. Cleverly, I brought hats, in order to avoid styling my hair. The less time I stood in front of the mirror the better off we were. I was so preoccupied with my looks and weight that joy had no place in my life. I never fully enjoyed my children or my husband, suffering in a world of my own– an ugly, hideous world that I could not escape. The obsessions with my looks continued to spiral out of control causing me to shrink farther away from life.

Rob, tried his best to help me overcome the obsessive compulsions, the torment I lived with daily. He was willing to take me anywhere, at whatever cost, searching high and low for a solution. We traveled from one hair salon to the next, hoping to find a simple cut that would free me from the preoccupation with my looks. Yet no special cut brought the relief I sought.

Living in anguish with no end in sight impaired my ability to live. Constantly battling against oneself is truly the worst war anyone can wage. Without hope of ever getting better, I came to a logical conclusion—I would be better off dead. *I would rather be dead. My husband and children will be better off without me. This torment is too hard to tolerate.* I decided to take my life. During an evening walk on the beach with Rob and the girls, I felt like a dead fish washed up on the shore. Christina and Stephine were running, laughing, playing in the sand, while I kept a distance. They were fully alive, but I was empty. It saddened me further to feel this way, knowing I tried my best to get well, yet still worsened. *There is no hope left for me.* After our evening walk on the beach, I went into my bathroom, downed all my medication, and simply went to bed. *They will no longer suffer from my bizarre behavior. I will no longer have to live in agony.* I looked forward to my death. Embracing it with pure joy and peace, knowing I'd be set free from the torment of living hell. Quickly, I faded away, lying alone on the bed.

When I slowly opened my eyes, bright lights shone above me. I realized I was still alive, lying in a hospital bed with Rob by my side. I have no clue how I got there. I had no idea they pumped my stomach out. Even though they pumped my stomach out, they demanded I drink two cups of black charcoal. They explained it was necessary in order to absorb any remaining medication. I did not want to live, and now I was forced to drink this awful looking stuff. The blackish gunk looked like something they had scooped from the bottom of a barbecue pit.

The doctor and nurses became upset when I refused to drink the dreadful stuff.

"Barb, please drink the stuff so we can go home." Rob begged. "They're not going to let you out of here unless you drink it. Just gulp it down as quickly as you can. The girls are waiting to go home."

The taste of the charcoal was hideous. Like drinking a cup of sand, laden with black tar. With each gulp, tears fell from my eyes. I kept telling Rob I did not want to be alive. He kept telling me to hush up or I would not be released. I sucked it up and finished drinking the dreadful cups of charcoal. They released me in Rob's care, impressing upon us the need for psychiatric treatment.

Upon arriving home, life carried on, but the conflict within me grew. I did not pursue additional psychiatric treatment, I was not ready to confront and release the skeletons from my past. I pressed on, carrying the grave cargo with me. I held a part-time job as a property manager. It was difficult working with this debilitating condition. The time at work wasn't the issue, it was the amount of time I spent in the bathroom preparing for work. Getting ready in the mornings was excruciating. Having the kids around, my mother-in-law coming over to baby-sit, and the war in front of the mirror was too much for me to tolerate. *I'll never get out of this bathroom on time! I look disgusting! Why did God make me so ugly?* Everyday I left home to go to work, filled with anxiety and paranoia. In my eyes, I looked hideous, ugly, revolting. In everyone else's eyes, I looked 'perfect'.

Unfortunately, my compulsions, distortions, and anxiety became too overwhelming. I turned to drinking in order to escape the pain. I looked forward to Fridays, knowing a six-pack of beer awaited me. This obviously did not work for very long, because what started as a once-a-week relaxation quickly invaded my weekdays too. The ugliness in the bathroom mirror grew uglier and I just did not understand why. The drinking allowed me to unwind, yet I knew it wasn't the answer to the problem. Rob continued to do anything and everything he possibly could to help me out, but I was so sick within myself, I couldn't accept his care and love. This confused me even more. I did not understand how I could love anyone when I could not even tolerate myself.

With so much turmoil brewing within, my judgment regarding many things became impaired. My marriage was suffering, my children were suffering, and my soul was trapped in some dark place. The solution to all my adversity was nowhere to be found. The prescription medication, alcohol, obsessive grooming, and exercise were all to no avail. Grasping for straws, a solution, any solution, I decided to move out of my home with Christina, leaving Rob and Stephine, behind in the condominium we owned. It broke my heart to make such a difficult decision, yet I justified my action, telling myself I was protecting them from my insanity. I believed this was the only way to do so. Honestly, I was too sick in the head to know better. I hoped getting my own place might alleviate the problems, but this decision nearly cost me my life again.

I did not realize I was setting myself up for a completely new set of problems. Things were fine for a little while, but then everything fell apart. I decided again that I needed professional help. I was battling with extreme highs and lows. It was such an odd feeling. One day I was living on top of the world, nothing was too hard for me to deal with. Life felt good–very, very good. Another day, all hope was lost. Death looked better than life. One day, I would see a beautiful image in the mirror and the next day, I would see the most hideous creature starring back at me.

With these extreme highs and lows taking place, I found a new doctor; he diagnosed me with Bipolar Depression. Immediately, he placed me on numerous medications to remedy my erratic behaviors. I hid the fact from him that I thought I was ugly. I felt uncomfortable telling him about the distortions, the battle in front of the mirror. I figured I had overloaded him with enough and he did not need this too. The medications he prescribed did not work. They only created additional confusion. *Should I take the medications? Should I drown these hideous thoughts and visions with alcohol? What reflection will I see in the mirror today?*

Sadly, the hideous images in the mirror increased and my drinking went to a new all-time high. Suicidal thoughts flooded back as well. Here we go again! History repeated itself. I found myself once again overdosing on prescription medicine in hopes of putting an end to the madness, the insanity.

When I tried to take my life the second time, I locked myself up in the bathroom and took every pill I had hoarded for months. I had not taken them according to direction, because they had not made the unsightly me go away. I remember my daughter, Christina, banging on the bathroom door to let her in. However, I refused. I kept yelling at her to leave me alone, that I wanted to be dead and she would be better off without me. She called 911 and told them to come out to our apartment. Soon after her phone call, the bathroom door burst opened. The individuals walking in were a blur to me. I dozed off in a daze as they grabbed hold of my arms. I blacked out.

Once again, I found myself still alive the following day, lying in a hospital bed. They had a twenty-four hour watch on me, because I was a high risk. *I don't believe I'm still alive! What a disgrace my life is. I want to be dead! At least I protected Rob and Stephine from experiencing this again, but I put Christina through so much more.* This suicide episode was worse than the first, the hospital refused to allow me to leave. The doctor who had been treating me gave up. He told me over the phone that my care was out of his hands and I needed to get a lot more help than what he had to offer. After spending several days in the hospital, they finally decided it was ok to release me. However, I had to follow-up with psychiatric treatment with the doctors they assigned.

Nobody got it! I could not take medicine, and they all wanted to keep medicating me. There was no solution to my adversity as far as I could see. What needed to be fixed within me could not be found in a stupid prescription bottle or a six-pack of beer. I felt like a guinea pig trying all sorts of medicines, at various doses, yet nothing worked. I had enough of the medicines and decided to stop cold turkey. Whether this was good or bad, I had no idea. I do know that once I stopped the medicines, my drinking ceased and the suicidal thoughts lessened as well. Little did I know some of the medications I took had adverse side effects that I was unaware of at the time. The side effects are often an increased desire for alcohol and the possibility of suicidal behavior. Go figure–two of the evils I was trying to overcome.

During my stay in the hospital, I realized I was not well enough to take care of my daughter, Christina. I decided to let her stay with my sister, Sandy, for a little while. I also gave up my apartment and moved back home to my husband, who was willing to work through the issues that were tearing us apart as a family unit. It hurt me a great deal not to be able to take Christina back home. However, I knew it was for the best, I still lived with too much distress within. I quit my job and concentrated on getting better so I could be a healthy mother and stable wife, too.

After several months of recuperating, I took a part-time bookkeeping job working at a woman's home. What started as something good, took a turn for the worse. This woman tried to dress me in a style I could not envision. She went away on business trips for weeks at a time and whenever she returned, she brought back gifts. I thought this was nice of her, but the gifts she brought back were inappropriate. Once she gave me sexy, black fishnet stockings, another time a black leather mini skirt. Not understanding why, what she wanted, left me very uncomfortable. Yet I needed the job.

Things were not working out well for me back home. The self-hatred, and evil memories buried within weren't allowing me to settle down no matter what I did. *Will I ever escape these gruesome memories? I feel dirty when Rob touches me. I'll never be a healthy wife.* I could not live with Rob and Stephine because I did not know how to live with myself, let alone anyone else. As a result, I decided to move back out. I wanted to spare them further bouts with my insanity, the inner war. In addition, I longed for Christina, but Rob did not think it was a good idea for her to return home yet. I found a nice rental nearby. Christina returned and we pushed on.

Father God, Pardon me for being an unwholesome mother and wife back then. Whatever heartache I brought upon my children, I ask that You forgive me and heal their hearts from whatever damages I might have inflicted upon them without even realizing it! Amen

- Have you ever thought about or perhaps tried to end your life?
- Have you been trying to "hide" issues from your past?
- Are you aware that your wrong choices and poor behavior can have an adverse effect on others, especially those you love?

Six

My Brush with Christ

When Christina and I settled into our own place, everything went smoother. My drinking stopped and the obsessions in the bathroom decreased greatly. *I don't feel suffocated anymore. No man is going to touch me. I finally have some alone time. I hope this will help me get better.*

In addition, due to an increase in my boss's business, my part-time job turned into a fulltime position. As a result, she relocated the business out of her house and into a regular office setting. I was excited when this occurred because I felt uncomfortable working from her home. The increase in pay allowed Christina and I to live independently. My self-esteem improved, because I recognized I had what it took to survive on my own. I really enjoyed working when my boss was away on business trips. It permitted me to be at ease, allowing me to perform more efficiently. However, when she returned, I felt on edge. She continued to manipulate me in regards to my attire. I always dressed appropriately, yet she continued to shove one clothing catalog after another in front of me, suggesting I ought to buy this or that. I felt inadequate, unable to live up to her standards. As I worked under her watch, she controlled every minute of my time. I grew to dislike the situation because of her obnoxious conduct. However, I needed the job in order to provide for my household. Therefore, I kept my mouth shut, continuing to perform to the best of my ability, no matter how rude she became.

As time passed, I coped well, managing my life and emotional health. I still fought the obsession regarding my appearance, yet it became more manageable with only Christina around. I even continued to help Rob attend to Stephine's needs. Living directly down the street allowed me to remain a part of her life. The distance served as a buffer, protecting her from my puzzled life. I remained abstinent from drinking and successfully proceeded to work each day, regardless of the fracas in the mirror. I still had no clue why this horrific condition continued to raise its ugly head, forcing me to live under its control. Continuing to conceal what I was undergoing on a daily basis became tricky. I knew nobody would understand the war I fought between the darkness that existed within me and the gruesome person appearing in my mirror. I hid the pain and sorrow in order to press on. What a masked, deceitful life I led!

After several months of living well on my own with Christina, I again succumbed to my inner turmoil. Something went wrong—terribly, terribly, wrong! The anxiety and suicidal thoughts stemming from the terror in the bathroom preoccupied my soul. The ugly image staring back flooded my mind with atrocious lies. *You are never going to get well! You will remain living with this hell! You will never escape and be free!* Sadly, I picked up drinking again, hoping to find relief. All I wanted was to escape from the monster in the mirror, the hideous lies bombarding my mind. Drinking allowed me to mellow out from the ugly lies, stemming from the images in the mirror.

Then one night my turbulent ways of living caught up with me. I could not handle my extreme highs, lows, and the stack of numerous conditions I juggled. I did not want to continue on the wild roller coaster any longer. I could not handle the disabling hours in the bathroom nor tolerate the self-destructive behavior-taking place. I felt ashamed of my life and needed the madness to end. One night, out of dire desperation, I called out to God. *"God, I don't want to wake up to see another day. I'd rather be dead! If you must keep me alive, then you have to help me get better. Please rescue me from this misery! God, let me die!"*

To my surprise, when I awoke the following morning, before even getting out of bed, I prayed to God to guide me into a church. It was Sunday morning, and for some odd reason I longed to be in His presence. I fought a dreadful conflict in the bathroom as I prepared myself to get ready. The tormenting obsessions nearly destroyed me. Yet, I survived the onslaught, the hideous grooming ritual. As I got into my car, a strange feeling encompassed me. I had no idea which church I was heading to, it was a spontaneous decision I made when I awoke. As I drove down the street, it felt as though a gentle hand chauffeured me. I pulled up along the side of an unfamiliar church. I hesitated for a moment, deciding whether to park my car or not. *Is this the one? Look at all the people. Will they stare at me because I'm ugly? Should I go in or not?* Within a few seconds, an incredible sensation stirred within—urging me inside. The overwhelming feeling was powerful. There was neither hesitation nor doubt. *This is the place! Yes, this is the church! I'm going in!*

As I journeyed towards the entrance, several parishioners greeted me with open arms. This made me feel welcomed, so relieved. I found a seat and immediately participated in the praise and worship taking place. I had never done this before, but my heart longed to connect. The songs were uplifting and joyous—ministering healing to my deprived soul. I cried as I joined in on the singing. If someone handed me a dollar for every tear I released, I'd been a millionaire. They were endless. Thank goodness, boxes of tissues were at hand. Tranquility entered my dilapidated soul—a blessed feeling no words could ever explain.

When the praise and worship session ended, I settled into my seat. Earnestly I waited for the pastor to take his stand at the podium, anticipating a well-needed sermon. I don't recall the exact message spoken, but it infiltrated my heart. As service was about to end, the pastor asked everyone to close their eyes and bow their heads for prayer. After a minute or two of prayer, with heads all bowed he asked, "Is there anyone who would like to accept Jesus Christ as their Lord and Savior? Please raise your hand."

Without hesitation, I raised my hand, lifting it as high as possible. I felt like a little girl in school who had the answer to a sought-after question asked by the teacher. I knew in my heart, right there and then, I needed Jesus Christ in my life. I had no idea the pastor was going to ask all of us, who raised their hands, to go up for additional prayer. Right away, I walked up to the front where the pastor was waiting with arms wide open. I trembled, as I stood in front of the sanctuary, grateful to be standing there. The pastor had me recite a special prayer, accepting Jesus Christ as my Lord. The moments were ever so precious.

Shortly after, elders of the church prayed over me. Tears of joy and sorrow poured out of me as we prayed together. It felt as though the darkness trapped within relinquished its hold on me. My entire body went numb as the shadows of darkness dissipated. I felt enlightened. I did not want to leave the special atoning place. *This is a blessing! A gift from God!* The night before, I prayed to be released from my misery, anticipating and looking forward to death. Instead, God offered me so much more—peace, joy, and serenity surpassing all understanding, as well as, the precious gift of eternal life.

"For he says, 'in the time of my favor I heard you, and in the day of salvation I helped you.' I tell you, now is the time of God's favor, now is the day of salvation." —2 Corinthians 6:2 (NIV)

As I walked towards my car, I felt different. *Wow! I do not feel dirty & ugly. I am not troubled! I feel like I am finally alive!* Before entering church, I'd felt like a filthy, stinking rag. Upon leaving, I'd turned into a clean, piece of white linen, basking outside on a clothesline all day long, with a new fresh fragrance transcending. The weighty drape, which blanketed me, lifted. For the first time, in my life, I saw vibrant colors outside, and I heard birds chirping in the air. I was walking in step with the song, Amazing Grace —"I once was blind but now I see…"

The awesome experience I stumbled upon while attending that particular church was foreign to me. There I was, a young woman in her early thirties, unaware that a church of that sort existed. The last time I stepped into a church was for my great-grandmother's funeral. Actually, as I sit here, writing this chapter, I recall the church I attended for Grandma Mary's funeral was the same church I attended when I was young. For some reason, my memory blanks out the bulk of the time I attended. Based on an old photograph, I made my first communion. The same holds true for my first confession. It's odd–I don't recall participating in those activities. To tell you the truth, I do not even know what their purpose was. For some reason my mind did not absorb the matter. I followed a so-called religious tradition without an understanding of what I was doing. I even had my daughter, Christina baptized in my childhood church when she was born. However, I had no perception of its purpose or significance. There again, I followed a religious tradition my family practiced. *Was my heart and mind that warped? Why was I unable to comprehend any of this stuff?* None of the old church stuff struck my heart the way this newfound church did.

I'll be the first to admit, I never understood God, Christ, or church. The word of God never penetrated my mind, heart, or soul. Maybe I was cursed, maybe because I was too immersed in all the evil and chaos that surrounded me. However, the new church God delivered me to lifted the veil from my heart, making me fully aware of His presence. I'm glad I didn't allow any childhood religious beliefs to cloud my mind, for I believe this allowed God to do what He desired to accomplish—for me to believe in His son, Jesus Christ, and accept Him as my personal Savior. I am blessed and grateful God delivered me to an awe-inspiring church when I needed it the most.

Clearly, upon leaving this church, something inside me vanished. I felt all cleaned up inside. The obsessions and anxiety in my bathroom disappeared. For the first time in years, I felt good about myself in a healthy way, not in a self-destructive manner. The barricaded walls around my heart collapsed. Finally, I began to enjoy life. It was, without a doubt, a total turn around. I didn't know that when the inside of someone is clean, then the outside stuff becomes naturally beautiful. I was a sinner, so lost, and filled with guilt and shame. No wonder I hadn't been able to look at myself in the mirror. I now finally looked at myself in the mirror and saw a beautiful, loving person gazing back, no longer haunted by the ugly, hideous reflection that tormented me.

During this awe-inspiring time, I made amends with my predator regarding the sexual molestation. One evening he phoned and explained that he was very troubled by the things he had done. Crying, he asked for forgiveness. Without hesitation, I accepted his apology and forgave him. I was thankful that God was healing me; in exchange, it allowed me to begin to forgive others.

I attended church on a weekly basis. In fact, I attended Bible study during the week as well. I could not get enough of what God wanted me to have and receive, His word and His truths. I felt like a newborn infant, feeding on its mother's milk. I needed to feed on the Word of God in order to live, grow, and mature. I started reading my Bible daily. I prayed more and more for my loved ones. I also attended church membership classes because I wanted to become a member of such a great family of believers. I began to break out of the shell I was locked up in for so many years. The greatest feeling anyone could ever experience—imagine a prisoner, set free after being wrongfully locked up for over thirty years.

"The Lord sets prisoners free, the Lord gives sight to the blind, the Lord lifts up those who are bowed down, the Lord loves the righteous." —Psalm 146:8 (NIV)

Father God, I am so grateful that You heard my prayer that night, when You came quickly and swiftly to my rescue. Lord Jesus, thank You for stepping into my life just when I was about to lose my mind and all hope of ever getting better. Your Light shone on my darkness and gave me new life! Without accepting You into my heart and life, I would not have received the gift of salvation...to be able to live in eternity with You. Thank You, Lord. In Jesus' name, Amen

---

- Do you know that Jesus is "the only way" for you to enter heaven and reside with God in eternity?
- Have you personally accepted Jesus Christ as your Lord and Savior? If not, there is a prayer at the end of this book that you can recite inviting Jesus into your heart and life.
- Do you comprehend the difference between following "religious traditions" verses enjoying and developing a "personal relationship" with the Lord?

Seven

The Enemy Steps In

Everything in my life was marvelous, until one day I faltered. If only I had known, I was stepping into a deadly entrapment. During this rebirth, I was not dating anyone. I fully devoted my time to the Lord and dedicated myself to getting my life cleaned up. I had neither desire nor interest in dating anyone—contentment reined my life. Happiness and joy followed me wherever I roamed, rays of sunshine transcending from within. Relationships with my beloved ones entered into a completely new realm. Where once I had been unable to love, now healthy nourishing relations grew in my life.

Then one day, my younger sister set me up on a blind date. I told her I wasn't interested because I was doing well with my life, yet I reluctantly agreed in order to pacify her. I half-heartedly arranged to meet him over a game of tennis the following day, using the net as a buffer. When he arrived, I remained hesitant. We went out to play tennis and I was stunned over how well the match went. Of course, I won! As a result, I decided to extend another engagement at the end of the workweek. We had a lot in common in terms of physical activities. I enjoyed working out on a daily basis and so did he. We participated in many fun-filled outdoor activities. As we grew to know each other, we developed a more serious relationship.

Soon after, a subtle concern stirred in my inner being, cautioning me. He didn't have the same spiritual relationship with Christ as I. However, he showed an interest in the Bible and in going to church as well. Thrilled to lead him, I soon felt an alarming conviction in my heart that he had no true interest in Christ. I believe he wanted to impress me in order to remain in my life.

Sad to admit, we began a more intimate relationship, which included sex. Because I felt convicted of wrongdoing, I felt smothered, dirty, and shameful again. Unworthy, I picked up drinking again. This behavior ought to have been a clear-cut warning sign. I was in danger, diving back into the pit of destruction and despair from which I had just escaped. I let it drag on and everything fell to ruins in my brand-new, cleaned-up life. Why didn't I heed the caution and warning signs more seriously? I wondered.

I suppose my lack of spiritual knowledge and wisdom, as well as fleshly desires thwarted my moral judgments. I was a so-called "baby Christian," neither yet developed or seasoned in God's word. I felt like a little lamb, snatched and dragged into the slaughterhouse. I lost touch with my Shepherd, my shelter. The enemy lured me back into sinister surroundings. My snow-white wool turned a deep shade of gray, making me feel like the black sheep. My green pasture turned into a frightening wilderness, a desert wasteland. I found myself back on the wild roller coaster.

"Be self-controlled and alert. Your enemy the devil prowls around like a roaring lion looking for someone to devour."
—1 Peter 5:8 (NIV)

The hurt, pain, and ugly distortions rushed back, more powerful than ever before! I felt torn in two as if I was in a boxing match with Satan himself. Good and evil existed within and I did not know how to escape. I lost my identity. I did not know whom I belonged to. Was I a child of God? Was I a creature of Satan? *Am I righteous or am I evil? I am so lost and confused!* One day blessed, and the next day cursed again. What a disgrace I allowed myself to become once again.

The ugly feelings and sightings that God banished, returned to an unusual extent. Living in disobedience to God, stepping into a sexual relationship drove me deeper into my misfortune. I did not understand why this strong conviction troubled me. I tried to drown the feelings and inescapable "truth" with alcohol, but it only brought more disaster. The images in the mirror grew uglier and I couldn't stand to look. The obsession in the bathroom took over my life once again, and I was unable to find any form of relief. No matter how perfect I kept trying to make myself look on the outside, the gruesomeness living inside still existed. I knew right from wrong now. I knew I was living in sin.

Filled with shame, I stopped going to membership classes and ceased attending church as well. I did not want to be a hypocrite. I knew I was not living up to God's expectations. I became the enemy's bait, trapped in a prison cell of the horror lodged within the mirror. I was a casualty of sin tortured daily by hideous distortions and condemnation. My life was joyful when it was only the Lord and I. However, when I allowed someone to coerce his way in, a wolf disguised in sheep's clothing snuck in. I believe God wanted me for himself at this precious, vulnerable time of my life. By continuing in this relationship, I opened myself up to Satan's control.

I lost complete control over my drinking. My addiction to alcohol and torments of self-hatred infected every area of my life. The forces of evil lurked throughout my mind and body like a raging inferno. Darkness ruled again. Clearly, I battled my old nature, the flesh, and my new nature, the spirit. My old ways of living and my new ways of living were clashing. I became frightened because I did not know how to win the battle taking place inside of me. The anxiety stemming from the obsession in the bathroom mirror hit an all-time record. My distorted mind persuaded me to run away from my troubles, which only led me to further destruction.

One evening, I decided to go out drinking, hoping to get away from the relationship that now suffocated me, and to flee from my tormented obsessions. I picked up a six-pack of beer and proceeded to suck it down within an hour. Highly intoxicated, I still craved more. I went to the nearest bar and ordered several more drinks. As I sat on the bar stool, watching everyone else enjoying themselves, thoughts of suicide invaded my mind. I could not get the nasty thoughts out of my head. I walked to the public phone and called Mom. Crying hysterically, I told her I was going to kill myself.

After talking with her for several minutes, I hung up the phone to leave. *Should I hang myself? Should I drive my car off the bridge? I wish I had a gun.* As I walked towards the car, several police officers and an ambulance pulled up beside me. They were aware of the suicidal mode I was in and tried to persuade me into the ambulance but I refused their help. After arguing with them for several minutes, I blacked out.

When I awoke, I realized I was back in the hospital, this time it was a mental ward. My suicidal condition was so bad; they locked me away for nearly three weeks. I could not wait to be released. It killed me to be around so many people. Most of the time, I remained silent and kept a distance. Some of the treatment helped, but it did not take away the ugly person I battled against, myself. *Why am I still alive? God get me out of this place.*

During the time in the hospital, I realized the relationship triggered my illness, and thus took the next step to recovery. I decided to step back from the relationship. I could not deal with the ugliness that came with it. A guilty conscience and memories of my molestation from childhood troubled me. I went back to seeing doctors and they placed me on several prescriptions–again!

Unfortunately, trying to live a life of make-believe and cover-up no longer worked. I didn't have the strength to maintain the facade. This horrible condition drained the life out of me. The obsessions, self-hatred, rage, and torment reached a climax. I will never forget one of the most agonizing days of my life while grooming. Hour, after hour trapped in the bathroom mirror trying to escape from the obsessions that held me captive. It was so ferocious I never made it to work. I was trapped in the 'torture chamber' for several grueling hours. By the time the eighth hour approached, my doctor phoned the house looking for me. We had a scheduled appointment that day and I did not show up for it. I remember Christina answering the phone when he called.

Guardedly, she said, "Mom, your doctor is on the phone. He wants to know if you are on your way to see him."

I reluctantly put down my styling stuff and took the phone from her. Our exact phone conversation is a blur, but once we finished speaking, I was able to step out of the bathroom for the remainder of the day. Sad to say, nearly nine hours had passed from start to finish. I lost all hope of ever getting better.

After combating this dreadful occurrence, my doctors acknowledged the severity of my condition. They highly recommended that I quit my job, knowing it contributed to the terror I fought in the bathroom. Actually, they were quite adamant, recommending I apply for Social Security Disability benefits. They knew I was not in any condition to be working under such atrocious mental anguish. Out of great concern, they suggested I see them three times a week in order to monitor my condition and medications more closely.

I followed their advice, quitting my job and applying for Social Security Disability benefits. These decisions were stressful, because I had no idea how I was going to make ends meet. What once was not an issue became a very anxious concern. *How will I pay my rent and utility bills? Will I be able to afford to put food on the table for Christina?* Shortly after this wondering, I realized that everything was going to work out fine as long as I committed to do my best in getting well. *Christina and I will be ok. God will provide. I need not fear nor be anxious.* Words implanted within my heart and mind while studying my Bible.

My doctors backed me up when I applied for disability benefits. I was not undergoing a physical impairment; rather it was a mind-boggling, mental condition. As far as I am concerned, mental disabilities are worse because no one can visibly see your abnormality, nor do they tend to believe it. My mind held me captive in an unlivable nightmare that was literally killing me. This time, my mental condition rapidly declined and fortunately, Social Security Administration allowed me to apply for benefits over the phone. Psychologically, I imprisoned myself within my own home. The obsessions and anxiety pending from the war within the bathroom mirror reached a highly toxic level of insanity.

"When an evil spirit comes out of a man, it goes through arid places seeking rest and does not find it. Then it says, 'I will return to the house I left.' When it arrives, it finds the house swept clean and put in order. Then it goes and takes seven other spirits more wicked than itself, and they go in and live there. And the final condition of that man is worse than the first." —Luke 11:24-26 (NIV)

My entire life was under the control of some evil force. A good comparison would be a scene from the movie, The Exorcist. *I'm living under a curse! What has been passed down to me? Will I ever escape from the evil that resides within me?* Nightmares took over where the torment in the bathroom left off. I believed satanic forces tried to suffocate me while I slept. I was trapped in a trance and I could not budge. The evil forces paralyzed me as I fought to break free. My wrists and ankles felt as if they were shackled to the bedposts. As the bed shook, as though a stampede of wild horses were underneath, I tried to shout to Christina, but was unable to. *Why can't I yell? Did someone tape my lips up?* It took every ounce of energy I had to fight the satanic attack off as I reached for my Bible on the nightstand. Trembling, I hung onto the cross around my neck, as I placed the Bible under my pillow in order to get back to sleep. At this point, I feared going into the bathroom and dreaded going to bed as well.

I knew applying for benefits and waiting for approval from Social Security was a daunting process. The representatives informed me how long the procedure could take—anywhere from six months to a year. Fortunately, I was eligible to receive state assistance during this process. It helped a bit, but wasn't enough to cover my monthly expenses. I still knew within my heart that God would provide, so long as I did my part. I stayed afloat by cutting back on spending, and became more frugal with my limited resources.

Visiting the doctors for scheduled appointments became more difficult. Most of the time, I never made it out of the bathroom. *I have to get to my appointment! I need to step away from this mirror! I am too ugly to go out!* This made matters worse because I knew I needed help. Bearing the agony of defeat the majority of the time tortured my inner core. I thought I had no other choice but to stop seeing them because I could not handle the distress. I became more and more suicidal each time I attempted to see them and failed. My obsession grew out of control, forcing me into making abrupt changes once again—a clean sweep of my entire life.

Father God, Pardon me for my failure to pay attention to and heave the warning signs Your Spirit was prompting me to. You graciously and mercifully cleansed my inner being when I accepted Your Son into my heart and life. However, I allowed the enemy to step in making my life even worse than before. Thank You for not giving up on me and for loving me enough to give me a second chance to make things right with You. Amen

---

- Do you realize you have a cunning enemy, Satan, who wants to destroy your relationship with God?
- Has God's Holy Spirit ever sent warning signs your way?
- If so, did you respond appropriately?

Eight

A Clean Sweep Again

I can't take life anymore. I have to stop all this turmoil. I'm pulling back from everything. I completely ended the relationship I was trying to cling to; I quit drinking, stopped seeing doctors, and discarded all my medications. *God, I'm sorry! Please take me back into your loving arms.*

> *"Count on it—there's more joy in heaven over one sinner's rescued life than over ninety-nine good people in no need of rescue."*
> —Luke 15:10 (TM)

I returned to church. Wow! Amazingly, I started to recuperate as I let go of the "things" I ran to, and rebuked the enemy from my sacred territory. I knew in my heart, the healing I longed for was going to come from God's mercy and love towards me. *Doctors cannot fix me. Medicine is not the solution. Men aggravate my debilitating condition.* Once again, life became brighter for Christina and me. I'm grateful my daughter, Stephine, didn't witness or live with my insanity. Thank God, she lived with her father while I struggled to be a decent, functioning mother. Living a block away gave me the ability to take part in what little ways I could muster.

Just when everything started to go smoother, the property owner decided to sell the condominium I was renting. I had to find a new home. This didn't trouble me, because I felt a new location might serve us well, granting us freedom to step away from the bad experiences we endured while living there. The condominium wasn't listed for more than a week, when I received notice it sold.

It was a blessing when Christina and I found our new place. The location was perfect, because it allowed Christina to remain in the same school and it permitted me to continue living near Stephine. The only drawback—we needed to wait one month for it to be ready. We packed our belongings and stored them in a storage unit for the month. Christina went to stay at a friend's house, while I stayed at a neighbor's home. It was hard for us to separate, but we had to do it in order to move on. My neighbor, Eileen, was an older woman from my church who ministered greatly to my needs. The alone time we had together brought healing to my broken spirit. The inconvenience of waiting for our new apartment turned out to be a two-fold blessing. I received well-needed godly counsel, and ultimately we received the perfect place to live as well.

Eileen, being a devoted woman of faith, became my spiritual mother during the course of my stay at her home. She taught me a lot about the Word of God and His unconditional love for me. She flooded my mind with book, after book, after book. Teaching me things, I had no understanding of, or insight into. One of the greatest lessons she taught me regarded tithing. I will admit, at first, it was hard to tithe, because of my financial circumstances. However, as I watched her, I developed moral habits as well. I was not receiving much at this point, but with the little I did receive, I stepped out in faith and tithed regardless, because I knew in my heart it was the right thing to do. I obeyed the counsel of the Bible that says, *"But seek first his kingdom and his righteousness, and all these things will be given to you as well."* —Mathew 6:11 (NIV)

It was well worth the wait when Christina and I moved into our new apartment. We were in glory when we walked into our new home for the very first time. *Wow! It's all remodeled. Everything is brand new. This is beyond what I prayed and asked for.* I knew God was watching over us. He was taking care of our needs, as long as I remained in right standing with Him. As I strived to live a righteous life, ghosts from the past and wrongful attitudes still-hunted me in the mirror at times. *Leave me alone. I am a new being in Christ. This is old stuff.* Reading my Bible daily, watching sermons on television, and listening to them via radio, brought spiritual nourishment to my mind and heart. All of this became my new means of getting well. God was healing me from the inside out.

Christina and I settled into our new apartment and things continued to go well. I felt blessed because I was doing my best in spite of the disabling situation. However, the obsessions continued to grow, giving me no choice but to start seeing doctors again. I believed that Satan was trying to keep me locked up under his control as I fought to escape and receive my healing. I was flip-flopping all over the place—trusting God for healing one day, running to doctors the next. I found a new set of doctors. My previous doctors informed of them my condition and they were eager to continue to assist me in obtaining Social Security Disability benefits, which were still in the review and approval process.

Once again, they placed me on several medications and scheduled me for weekly visits, just like my former doctors. I was repeating things all over again, but this time I was hopeful of a full recovery. The doctors were specialists in the area of obsessive-compulsive behavior. One of them had me working on several coping techniques, dealing with my fear and compulsions. One coping technique was for me to place a one-hour timer in the bathroom. When it ran out of time, I was to leave the bathroom regardless of whether or not I was done with my grooming ritual. This was a huge challenge because I averaged, on a good day, anywhere between three to four hours. They also had me keep an account of how much time I spent in the bathroom, how high my anxiety levels were, and how long it took to calm down. It was nerve racking to say the least, but it brought a great deal of insight. The techniques allowed me to recognize when I was improving and when I was slipping, what situations increased my paranoia, and when I felt more at ease.

Living on a limited income while waiting for the approval of my disability benefits forced me to apply for energy assistance. I had to go to the Town Hall in order to apply for the extra financial help. I was embarrassed over needing to apply, but I had to in order to have heat for the winter. As I waited patiently for the intake worker, I stumbled across a brochure, which caught my attention. The title on the front page read, "How to deal with Body Dysmorphic Disorder" otherwise know as BDD. I had no clue what BDD stood for and out of curiosity I read the literature. I was blown away by the discovery, because it described my disabling condition to a T. The "ugly" disorder terrorizing my life had a name. Everything within the brochure described what I faced. The following information from the internet provided by the *Mayo Clinic* will give you further insight to the disorder:

Definition by Mayo Clinic staff

Body Dysmorphic disorder is a type of chronic mental illness in which you can't stop thinking about a flaw with your appearance — a flaw either that is minor or that you imagine. But to you, your appearance seems so shameful and distressing that you don't want to be seen by anyone. Body Dysmorphic disorder has sometimes been called "imagined ugliness." When you have Body Dysmorphic disorder, you intensely obsess over your appearance and body image, often for many hours a day. You may seek out numerous cosmetic procedures to try to "fix" your perceived flaws but never are satisfied.

Risk factors: Although the precise causes of Body Dysmorphic disorder isn't known, researchers have identified certain factors that seem to increase the risk of developing or triggering the condition, including:

- Having biological relatives with body dysmorphic disorder

- Childhood teasing

- Physical or sexual abuse

- Low self-esteem

- Societal pressure or expectations of beauty

Complications: Body Dysmorphic disorder may cause or be associated with include:

- Suicidal thoughts or behavior

- Depression and other mood disorders

- Anxiety disorders

- Obsessive-compulsive disorder

- Eating disorders

- Social phobia

- Substance abuse

- Low self-esteem

- Social isolation

- Difficulty attending work or school

- Lack of close relationships

- Becoming housebound

It felt as though I was reading the story of my life and the hopes of getting better emerged more and more. I felt like a little girl who just grabbed the brass ring. I left the office feeling relieved, happy, and doubly blessed. Not only did the energy assistance go through, but I received insight as to what I was facing.

I didn't know how or who could possibly cure me from this disorder because I suffered from almost all the risk factors and complications listed above, which are additional diseases in their own right. Knowing it had a completed-suicide rate more than double that of major depression frightened me. I tried to end my life three times already, but from which one of the culprits?

Shortly after, I received notice in the mail that my Social Security disability went through. I thanked God for everything that was taking place. I knew in my heart He was working behind the scene. He knew my heart was traveling in the right direction and I was doing my best to hang in there and survive. Day in and day out, I would go down to the beach, early in the morning, weather permitting, and pray to God to help me get better. *God, please get me better. God, please set me free to be the real me.* I always prayed for Him to protect my children from my adversity. All I desired was to get better, so I could be a good mom. So long as I sustained in doing the proper things that needed to be done, His healing would take place. Sure enough, things continued to improve and I remained optimistic, as long as I remained by myself and allowed God to work within me.

As time passed, my doctor suggested I enroll in school, rather than staying isolated at home. She wanted me to challenge my fears in the bathroom and get to places on time, overcoming the paranoia. Knowing I would have to groom myself before classes and get to school on time, I gave it a lot of thought. Hesitantly and with great trepidation, I agreed to comply with her recommendation. I enrolled in an accounting program at the local community collage. I chose accounting because I enjoyed working with figures. One of my biggest concerns was the fact I did not know how to write well—another hidden flaw I dealt with. I knew I would have to take a few writing courses improving my skills. Regardless, I went ahead and enrolled.

Sure enough, I started the school year off with a full course load, thinking I was ready to handle it. I will admit it was very challenging. Not only was I battling with my obsessions, but I also concealed the fact I was on disability. *They will laugh in my face if I tell them I think I am too ugly to be alive.* It was tough because often I would go to school flagged with suicidal thoughts stemming from the "ugly" bathroom mirror. This condition interrupted my concentration in class because I did not feel comfortable sitting around others. I felt hideous and out of place. Whenever I encountered bad days in the bathroom, the distortions played havoc in my mind. Often, as soon as I settled down into my classroom chair, I would pull out sheets of paper and begin writing prayers to God. *Dear God, Please HELP! Please get rid of these ugly thoughts. Calm me down so I can listen and learn.* There were a few days of relief when I did not believe I was ugly. Without those days, I likely would not have made it through the first semester.

"I found myself in trouble and went looking for my Lord; my life was an open wound that wouldn't heal."
—Psalm 77:2 (TM)

It was a relief when the first semester ended. I needed a break from the "ugly image" stalking me from within my mirror. I was delighted when I saw my name on the honor roll. I knew the amount of hard work I had put into my studies, in spite of my debilitating mindset. As a result, I decided to continue to challenge myself by enrolling in an additional full course load the following semester.

Father God, Thank You for providing for Christina and I. Miraculously, we remained afloat while pushing forward in life. I praise You for all the good days I encountered in spite of the disorder that tried to keep me locked up. I thank You for the hedge

60

of protection You placed around me each time I went to school. Abba, You are truly amazing! Amen

---

- Are you familiar with Body Dysmorphic Disorder (BDD)?
- Are you currently battling with it yourself?
- Do you perhaps know someone that is suffering from it?
- Have you been struggling with any of the other issues listed? If so, have you sought help?

"I love GOD because he listened to me, listened as I begged for mercy. He listened so intently as I laid out my case before him."

—*Psalm 116:1-2 (TM)*

Nine

Opening of a Once Closed Door

With things going right in my life, I believed I traveled the road to recovery. I knew the name of my disease, the doctors were treating me, I was attending school, I had my Social Security disability to pay my bills, and my connection with God was steadfast. However, I felt lonely and began talking with the person I was previously seeing. Foolishly, I opened the door to the relationship I had ended several months prior. I was naïve, thinking I was well enough to allow him back into my life. I inadvertently opened up Pandora's Box all over. The evils that fled when I ended the relationship the first time quickly reappeared. *We are back! You are not going to escape from us this time!* Guilt, shame, and disgust penetrated my mind, heart, and soul. Most of all, I detested the ever increasing demoralizing reflection looking back at me in the mirror. Restarting this former relationship, my inner being destabilized rapidly. I felt smothered and dirty again, and my wild roller coaster took off with vengeance. History repeated itself.

> *"They prove the point of the proverbs, "A dog goes back to its own vomit," and, "A scrubbed-up pig heads for the mud."*
> —2 Peter 2:22 (TM)

The conflict within me became unbearable. I felt ashamed dragging my teenage daughter Christina back into my illogical world. I could not stomach looking at myself in the mirror. *You are ugly. You are a bad mom. You are better off dead.* Often, I wanted to smash my head into the mirror, hoping to put an end to the crazy thoughts ravaging my mind. *I am sinning against God. I should not be in this immoral relationship. Why did I open this once closed door?* Instead of letting, my relationship with God grow, I had gone back to an immoral relationship, which should have remained closed. I was in the middle of a battlefield "the good, the bad, and the ugly" all at war. I desperately needed to escape from the incompatible worlds, life sources trapped within.

At this critical junction, I knew I was in serious trouble. I knew I drifted away from God again and needed to get back on track. In an effort to follow the Lord's path, I ended the relationship again. A bit of comfort came as soon as I let go. I continued to see my doctors, continued to attend school, yet my struggle with the adversities I faced in the bathroom grew steadily. As a result, my doctor requested I lighten my course load. The BDD progressively interfered with my ability to get to school each day. I knew I was at a snapping point of suicide again. Sadly, the torture in the bathroom progressively worsened every time I had to groom myself for either school or a doctor's appointment.

I will never overlook the suicidal thoughts that clouded my mind driving toward school that semester. Plans to drive off the top of the parking garage entered my mind. Many times, I drove to the top of the parking garage prepared to drive off and end the torment. However, I would think about my daughters and would return down to the lower level of the garage to safety. I knew evil forces were driving me, trying to destroy me, yet I also believed in my heart God kept me alive for a good purpose.

"The Lord has chastened me severely, but he has not given me over to death." —Psalm 118:18 (NIV)

By no means will I forget the times I had wandered down the hallways of school, stuck in a trance. It's an unbelievable feeling to be walking while everyone else is passing you by, and you feel as though you are wrapped up in some sort of a bubble. During episodes such as this, I would flee to the nearest bathroom and hide in the stalls until the fear and paranoia subsided. Often I thought I was losing control of my thinking. Not only was I held captive to my distorted ways of thinking at home, but also now, they were getting worse no matter where I went. It was all too much for me to bear and I was grateful to take my doctors advice. I dropped two of my classes at school. Two less days I had to venture out!

Regardless of the doctor's assistance, therapy, and prescribed medications my condition continued to deteriorate. By this point, the litany of disorders in my file weighed more than I did. A short recap— childhood trauma, father committed suicide, trapped in burning house, molested, bullied and traumatized in middle school, pregnant before graduation, beaten and almost killed by my first lover. I think everyone would agree my background was dysfunctional. Also, an assortment of diagnosis's over the years included anorexia, post partum depression, substance abuse, chronic depression, body dysmorphic disorder, obsessive-compulsive disorder, social phobia, post-traumatic stress syndrome—just to name a few. Yet I still struggled to survive each day.

My doctors offered me a new program that dealt with multiple diagnoses. Desperate, I accepted and made it to my first visit. Driving to the orientation session was excruciating. As paranoia and anxiety thrashed through my entire being, thoughts of driving into a tree or building with my feet pressing the pedal to floor intruded the entire trip.

As I sat through the session, all my hope plummeted. The program required my attendance several times a week. I knew the struggle was more than I was capable of overcoming. The agony, the pain, the suffering through the BDD in front of the mirror would surely crush me. It would be a death sentence. *God, surely there has to be a better way for me to get well.*

Dear God, Thank You for Your disciplining hand in my life, which caused me to recognize my error and folly. I apologize for my slip-up in reestablishing a relationship that You desired for me to end. Thank You for not allowing the enemy of my soul to thwart Your wonderful plans for my life. Although deadly thoughts of suicide tried to take me out, You protected me time and time again. Amen

---

- Have you ever tried to reopen a once-closed door to a relationship or something else that God wanted you to keep shut? If so, what happened?
- Have you been toiling with the idea of opening a closed door?
- Has God's disciplining hand been at work in your life lately? If so, are you ready to make whatever changes He is asking of you?

"Heal me, O Lord, and I will be healed; save me and I will be saved, for you are the one I praise."

—Jeremiah 17:14 (NIV)

Ten

Pull Back from Doctors

I pulled the plug once again. I quit seeing doctors and ceased taking the prescribed medications. I informed my therapist by phone that there was no way I could participate in the dual diagnosis program she suggested. I told her I was going to try to get better on my own, without further support from her office or the other facility. She advised me it was not a wise decision and expressed I needed acute help handling my severe condition. Adamant, I told her I could not deal with the stress of going to appointments and hated taking all the "crazy" medications. She reluctantly accepted and said if I needed her in the future, she would be available.

Thank goodness the disability payments continued. I acknowledged the fact I was incapable of working a fulltime job. However, I knew I needed additional income to make ends meet. I decided to apply for a part-time, seasonal pool job available at the residential complex where I resided. I would be working in compliance with the terms of Social Security Disability guidelines, which allow people collecting disability the opportunity to re-enter the workplace. I received the part-time, seasonal position, and hoped it was a good step in the right direction—in terms of trying to work. One main reason I thought I would be able to handle this particular job was because I did not have to shower or groom before going over to the pool. Another plus—I did not have to worry about driving to work filled with suicidal thoughts. The job was in walking distance. To some extent, I was avoiding the tormenting confrontation with the BDD, yet I knew I needed to challenge myself, if only with baby steps.

I performed my job well, tending to the daily duties. I kept the pool clean and a watchful eye on the patrons entering and exiting. I felt good knowing I was providing a clean, safe environment for the residents to come and enjoy. However, the daily social contact with them became increasingly disturbing because of the paranoia with my looks. I was troubled that I was not the "healthy" individual they presumed me to be. To them my outward appearance looked picture perfect, yet the image inside me was twisted and disfigured. The only way I continued doing the job was by hiding behind sunglasses, visors, and hats. I masqueraded around with props, trying to camouflage my distorted outward appearance. No pun intended, more or less, I was placing band-aids over my crippling mindset regarding my looks. I continued to believe I was unsightly. I did not understand why anyone wanted to associate with me. The more I kept my distance, the more they flocked to my side—as though I was a beam of light and encouragement. The mask I hid behind in the presence of others held up well. I walked around with a painted smile on my face at all times. This was my way of covering up the fact that I was dying inside and was not the victorious well-adjusted individual they perceived.

Nobody knew I was on disability—not even my boss. I was embarrassed by the fact, because I knew they would not understand—thinking I was off my rocker. However, there was an old, kindhearted man who I chose to confide my hidden troubles. John became a blessing. If not for him, I would never have made it through the season. I was downright honest with him regarding my distorted way of thinking. He truly took it all to heart and read up on the disabling BDD terrorizing my life. He wanted to have all the knowledge he could get in hopes of helping me continue my job. He knew the residents, enjoyed the fact that I worked there and wanted to make certain I would hold up through the daily demands placed upon me.

Often I made it to the job, only to find myself weeping my heart out to dear, old, John. Expressing to him how terrible I felt in regards to my looks and the present thought of suicide. Talking with him often lifted my spirits and helped release the fear and anxiety locked up inside of my mind. It was a blessing that he was around most of the time, because without his insight and support I would not have survived the summer. He lived in the same complex and we became dear neighbors.

I enjoyed and respected his company to the highest degree. He was an angel sent by God to help and protect me from the evils lurking everywhere. He was not paid to go to the poolside each day, but he made it his mission to be there every time I was scheduled to work. I never thought or imagined I would find such a dear friend. He was just an old, caring man who would lay down his life for me or anyone else for that matter. I did not have a lot of extra money, yet I always had just enough, so I could show my appreciation to him. I knew he lived on a tight income and had a sweet tooth as well. He enjoyed desserts from one of the local bakeries and I took pleasure in spoiling him with a few sweet indulgences—my way of giving back. My dreary days quickly turned into brighter ones after fulfilling such acts of kindness. The smile on his face whenever I brought him treats was very therapeutic to my soul. There was no doubt in my mind that God ordained that the two of us were to cross paths in order to become a blessing to each other.

Eventually my disability thwarted my ability to remain on the job and I gave up the position. Depression over the fact I was not well enough to finish the part-time job settled over me like a mantel of doom, especially since I had only a few weeks left. However, I knew I teetered on the edge of breaking apart again, and had no choice but to pull back. My classes at school were going to start up again within a few weeks, and I wanted to be ready. My decision to give up the part-time employment ended up being a blessing to good, old John. My boss accepted the fact I was not going to finish the season and agreed when I suggested he hire John for the remainder of the job. John was experienced due to the time he spent with me. It allowed him to finish the job for the rest of the season, which gave him peace of mind in knowing he would have extra income to pay his rent. It was a blessing to witness how nicely this situation fell into place for all of us—John, my boss, and me. God truly worked in a marvelous way as He strategically planned it all out.

"And we know that in all things God works for the good of those who love him, who have been called according to his purpose."
—Romans 8:28 (NIV)

With the pool job behind me and a few weeks to recuperate, I hid from everyone—especially from the hideous reflection in the bathroom mirror. This allowed me time to get my irrational thoughts under control before starting back to school. During my time of isolation, I focused my attention on God and His word. This always brought great relief and restoration to my dilapidated soul.

Fear provoked me as I prepared myself for the first day of school, not knowing if I would have a good day in the bathroom or a bad one. I struggled, yet I surmounted the tiresome grooming ritual and made it out of the house with no thought of suicide. I was happy that I made it to my classes as well as I did. However, as each day passed the BDD grew more and more out of control. I was often so distressed that no matter what was being taught I was unable to comprehend it. Anxious thoughts swirled around in my head distracting me from learning. As a result, I studied a great deal on my own at home. Even though I still fought the grueling obsessions in the bathroom, I did my best to get through yet another semester. I prayed constantly during the semester for relief from the agony building up inside of me. Fortunately, it seemed as though each semester ended just in the knick of time, providing me a well-needed respite.

The summer approached and my former boss called and asked if I would like to work for him again. I decided to try working the pool job for another season. I knew I was a little better, as I'd allowed God to restore me. It was good timing; my classes had ended and I knew I would not do well sitting around doing nothing. School kept my mind busy, even though I battled with the BDD. It also gave me a greater assurance of a brighter future for Christina and me if I could conquer my debilitating mindset. Therefore, taking on the pool job allowed me to feel as though I was making progress, and the extra income allowed me to continue to make ends meet.

Experiencing some signs of liberation from the BDD allowed me to plan a one-week vacation to Vermont to visit my sister, Debby, before starting the pool job. I brought both of my daughters with me and we all had a marvelous time. We laughed, we cried, and we had a fun time. However, as the week progressed, I was anxious to return to my quiet apartment. It was nice to visit, but I needed a break from all the chatter and commotion. I looked forward to returning to Connecticut so I could go down to the beach and enjoy a nice sunny walk. My body had enough of Vermont's frigid weather.

As I neared home, I sensed God watching over me, lifting the cold, dreary weather, and breaking out the well-needed sunshine that I desperately desired. I dropped Stephine off at her house and proceeded to my place. Joy and excitement twirled within my spirit when I got out of the car to stretch my legs from the long drive. I did not even unpack my bags from the trip because I was so eager to get to the beach for my evening walk before sunset. A glorious feeling dwelled within me that evening as I headed down to the beach. My smile was authentic. The phony, fake one I often carried fell to the wayside. I felt blissfully happy like a radiant beacon of light. Gratefulness branched from my heart because I knew God was hard at work in my life, healing, protecting, and blessing my loved ones and me, provided I remained close to Him and shunned my old ways of living in rebellion and disobedience to Him.

All year long, I continuously fed on the Word of God, prayed, and sought after Him. It was certainly paying off. I found myself attending church once again. This alone brought additional hope and comfort in the knowledge that my debilitating mindset was improving. As the pressures, stemming from the BDD gradually lifted, and the hideous image within my bathroom mirror steadily faded, I realized my heart and mind were heading in the right direction. I could make it through the bathroom ordeal and not "think or view" myself as an ugly person.

"He heals the brokenhearted and binds up their wounds."
—Psalm 147:3 (NIV)

Father God, I thank You for the God ordained friendship between dear old John and me. Without doubt, You destined our paths to cross. Thank You for preserving my relationship with my daughters. I praise You for all the special times I spent with them without turmoil brewing within me. Surely, traveling on the path of Your choosing pays off well. Joy, freedom, peace, and the presence of Your Holy Spirit are just a few of the wonderful things You give to those that choose to walk on the narrow path that leads to life. Amen

---

- Has God blessed you with a special friend just when you needed help and encouragement the most?
- When life becomes stormy, do you seek shelter under the almighty wings of God?
- How has your self-worth been lately?

"I sought the Lord, and he answered me; he delivered me from all my fears. Those who look to him are radiant; their faces are never covered with shame."

— Psalm 34:4-5 (NIV)

Eleven

Caution! Caution! Caution!

One must keep a watchful eye during times of growth, healing, and revitalization. All it takes is one wrong move, one misstep, and everything gained may fall to ruins. I am living evidence. I inadvertently walked into a seemingly harmless encounter, which diverted me from the righteous path I traveled. The caution signs were all there, yet I did not take them seriously and ended up back on the "wild roller coaster" yet again. I knew I wanted to follow God's path, somehow Satan kept tempting me away. My judgment regarding decision-making still lacked sureness.

This innocent encounter took place during my evening walk down on the boardwalk at the beach. Without reflection, I graciously passed by a man who also walked the boardwalk, but was traveling in the opposite direction. However, filled with joy and happiness during my second pass, I innocently asked how many times he had walked around the boardwalk. I was a bit curious because I had never seen him before. I assumed it was because I normally walked the boardwalk early in the morning and yet today I walked in the evening. With a serene, gentle voice, he said he went around six times. We chatted a few moments and carried on our own ways.

During my drive back home, I caught myself thinking about him. *He seems like a nice man. I wonder if I will ever see him again.* It was a strange thought, as I had no intention in establishing a relationship with anyone. I had already decided not to start a new friendship with someone of the opposite sex. I knew in my heart that I was not well. God was still hard at work repairing my wounded soul. Therefore, I left the idea alone, not giving it further thought the rest of the night.

The following morning I looked forward to my habitual morning walk down at the beach. I enjoyed early mornings because I typically read my Bible and wrote in my prayer journal before walking. The ritual was a vital part of my healing and proved to be working well–better than going to dozens of doctors. I settled down on my favorite boulder jetting out into the ocean, pulled out my Bible and prayer journal from my tote, and began my morning devotional time with God. When done, I packed my belongings, placed them into my car, and began my walk. Oh! What a delightful journey! I made my way around the boardwalk breathing in the fresh cool air. I traveled my usual six laps, totaling three miles. In a state of bliss, I decided to walk around one additional time. As I finished the final lap, I headed back to my car. Sure enough, I spotted the man I had bumped into the night before. He was gearing up to begin his walk.

Knowing he spotted me and not wanting to be impolite, I went over to say good morning before leaving. He noted it was too bad I had already finished my walk. Still energized, I thought it would be nice to walk some more so I decided to accompany him. It was pleasant, and we both enjoyed chatting with each other as we strolled. During our walk, I sensed an attraction and compatibility with him. I was surprised because I was not searching for a relationship. However, the calmness of his voice as well as his mannerisms attracted me. I knew he was older by his graying hair, yet it did not bother me. An hour later our walk finally ended and we thanked each other for the company before going on our own separate ways.

As I proceeded home, I could not help but to think about the lovely time I had walking with him. It was nice because it was an unintended encounter. In order to enjoy the simplest things of life, such as a pleasurable walk at the beach with someone, I believed everything had to be spontaneous. I had grown accustomed to living life this way. Whenever an activity had an appointed day or allotted time set, I panicked over the thought of battling with the taunting BDD. I never knew if I would make it to the event, appointment, or occasion. For this reason, impromptu living suited me best, allowing me to enjoy life—a delightful morsel at a time.

However, once I returned home, reality seeped into my consciousness and I sensed a feeling of doom. Fear and panic twirled around in my head at the thought of seeing Dave again. I trembled as I walked into the bathroom, envisioning the repulsive BDD heaving its ugly head—my reflection in the mirror.

This saddened me, because all I wanted was to overcome the BDD so I could live a happy, normal life like everyone else. Conversely, I did not realize I longed to get better for the wrong reason. I believe I should have sought to get well so God could use me for His purpose. Back then, I had no idea of my calling, I was still too immature in my walk with Christ to understand. This was not apparent to me until I was halfway through the writing of this book. I was too eager to be set free from the sheltered lonely place I had been in for so many years. I felt quarantined.

The BDD in the bathroom erupted viciously the same day I ended my walk with my newfound friend, Dave. The distress, the torment was dreadfully shocking as I groomed myself, hoping to enjoy the rest of the day. Instead, I quickly found myself struggling once again without hope of ever getting better. As a result, I took another death-defying dive. I was heartbroken, crushed, and afraid. *I will never overcome this BDD. I will always remain captive to this disabling condition.* I knew my distorted mindset this particular day was way out in left field. Yet again, I considered ending my life. The speed of my reversion into my old pattern of thinking terrified me. Right there and then, I knew I was still deeply mentally ill and there was no possible way I was going to drag another innocent bystander into my psychosis. The mere thought of a friendship with him frightened me. I knew I was ill and I could not see past my infirmity.

Hour after hour trapped irrationally grooming, propelled me back into starring at the gruesome image terrorizing me in the mirror. *Is God sending me a warning? Is Satan playing tricks on me? What caused this anarchy again?* Tossed into ailing omen, I finally escaped the torture chamber in the bathroom. My life was on the line at this crucial time, as I was exhausted fighting off the temptation to checkout of life. The thought of suicide soared and fogged up my mind to an alarming degree. I refused to leave my home, not trusting myself to encounter anyone.

I reverted into isolation, giving myself time and solitude in order to calm down and work on my recovery. In an effort to recover, I gave up my early morning walks at the boardwalk in order to avoid running into Dave, who I had met prior to my relapse. I dropped out of society for a few weeks hoping to bring my thoughts to a more logical level. I felt terrible taking such a step back. I know I missed the opportunity to spend quality time with my beloved ones and the mere handful of friends I had. I hid the worst of my condition behind the "shell" I lived in. My daughter, Christina, and I did our best to survive this storm.

*"Trust in the Lord with all your heart and lean not on your own understanding; in all your ways acknowledge him, and he will make your paths straight." —*Proverbs 3:5-6 (NIV)

I relinquished all of my concerns to God—allowing Him total control. As each day passed, I improved. I no longer considered taking my life and began to sense it was safe, ok for me to venture outside again. Hope returned to me once again, as I turned to God and his Word to see me through the horrifying storm. I thank God I recovered within a few weeks, because I was due to start back at the pool job. I thought this would be a good opportunity to try to work beyond the BDD. Stepping out in faith and trying to work this part-time job again made me feel a bit better about my situation. Even though I knew hiding behind hats and sunglasses was avoiding the BDD, I was still functioning. My self-esteem slowly returned and I was anxious to get back to my early morning walks at the beach. I did not expect to see Dave, assuming he no longer walked down there. Yet the very first morning I resumed my walk, he happened to be there as well. *Oh my! Dave is here.*

Father God, I praise You for having a watchful eye on me all the time. Thank You for Your Holy Spirit and the warning signs You sent my way. It is amazing how quickly You step in to protect Your children from harm. I am grateful I stepped back and ran directly to You for cover. Thanks for keeping me safe and restoring my soul. In Jesus' name, Amen

---

- Do you realize the importance of being cautious concerning all things that come into your life, even things that seem innocent and/or good?
- Have you ever written a letter to God about your struggles?
- If not, perhaps now is the time for you to start penning a personal letter to Him.

Twelve

Watch Your Step

My self-esteem was higher than normal during my first morning walk down at the beach. I felt I had been given a new lease on life during the time I spent in isolation. I knew God had lifted me from the "mire" I was in as I turned to Him as my source of help. Filled with immeasurable bliss, it felt like I was stepping into paradise. I cheerfully looked forward to my first morning walk in weeks. Talk about extremes! Obviously, my feelings and emotions were all over the place—highs, lows, and everything else under the sun.

As soon as I spotted Dave walking on the boardwalk mixed feelings churned within me. Fear as well as joy twirled around; anxiety due to the mayhem I'd just recovered from, and gladness over my feelings regarding him. Joy surpassed the fear and I found the courage to accompany Dave. I was astonished at the enjoyment I felt walking and talking with him. The remarkable serenity of his voice allowed me to feel at ease in his presence. Yet, during our walk, I wondered what he thought. *Does he think I am ugly? I wonder if he likes me or not?* Before our walk ended, we agreed to meet the following morning for another walk.

When I departed, I immediately considered the BDD playing head games with me again and the havoc which always followed. I did not know what would come of this relationship or what would transpire from my annoying condition. I had grown weary of my disabling circumstances and the alienation I lived in. Thus, I was willing to take a risk and attempt a new friendship based upon my current level of existence. Mind you, I was in a state of euphoria at this time. No darkness prevailed.

I will admit I did not expect the relationship to blossom as quickly as it did. Each time Dave and I met in the morning to walk, I became more attracted to him. Odd as it was, just several weeks prior, I had lost all hope of getting well. I felt embarrassed telling Dave about the distorted mindset I battled, yet I knew I had to inform him immediately. I did not wish to mislead him into thinking I was a healthy person. When I told him about my disturbing condition, I also expressed my hopefulness in surmounting it. I expressed how full of faith I was in God healing me. I am not certain whether or not he took me seriously, nor did I know if he fully understood how serious my condition could become. He only viewed my outward appearance and the enlightened state of wholeness I currently possessed.

A few weeks after meeting one another for morning walks, we decided to go out for an evening meal at a local pizza parlor. I knew I placed myself in a challenging position regarding the obsessions in the bathroom, yet I was willing to give it a fighting chance. As the late afternoon approached, I began to fret over having to shower, groom, and head out in time to meet Dave. The hours before the appointed time were grueling and extremely difficult to get through. The agonizing BDD ritual slammed into fast forward as I prepared myself in front of the mirror. *I am too ugly to go out. Will I make it there on time? I only have a few minutes left.*

Without a minute to spare, I made it to the pizza restaurant right on time. As I crossed the street, Dave pulled up in front of the restaurant and we walked in together. Feelings of paranoia and anxiety pulsed through me. Luckily, I found ease in Dave's presence and it did not take too long to unwind from my vexing demeanor.

When he removed his sunglasses, the radiant sparkle from his eyes captivated my heart. While we chatted, all sensations of distress from the BDD dissipated rapidly. We enjoyed one another's company so much we decided to lengthen our date. After the pizza, we took a wonderful stroll and enjoyed a movie. Afterward, he drove me home, walked me to the door, taking his stance with a handshake and a gentle hug.

Mind you, at this pivotal time, I remained very devoted to the Lord and continued to rely on Him to heal me from the inside out. I knew my prolific faith in God was slowly delivering me from my twisted mindset, and would ultimately set me free from captivity. Adhering to my spiritual unity with God and remaining steadfast in His Word widened my boundaries of living. This granted me the ability to see Dave on a steadier basis and not be boggled down by the crippling frame of mind I was accustomed to.

This truly was one of the best times of my life. To go on dates with Dave and not be caught up in the "ugly mirror syndrome" was a miracle in and of its self. I had not experienced this freedom in a long time. Actually, the only other time I experienced it was when I accepted Christ as my Lord and Savior, approximately two years prior to meeting Dave. We quickly fell in love with one another, our love growing stronger and stronger each day. It seemed like my prayers and petitions of becoming whole were finally coming true.

My daughter, Christina, now nearing eighteen, was preparing to move out to have her own apartment. As the time approached for Christina to move out, I decided to downsize my apartment to a more affordable one. There were several smaller units available within the complex I resided in.

As we spent most of our time together, Dave asked if I would like to move into his house instead of relocating into a new rental. At first, I was very apprehensive because I was not certain if remnants of the BDD would surface and spiral out of control again. He had no clue how brutal my condition could become since he had not been exposed to the wicked disorder. For the most part, it remained dormant during our early stages of dating. I thought everything might work out fine since it seemed to be under control and I adored him. I went ahead and took the plunge, moving into his house. In hindsight, I realized I messed up by not seeking God for wisdom and guidance before making such a move.

It took me awhile to adjust to my new living arrangement. I had been living on my own for quite a few years. A strange feeling troubled me with not having my own place any longer. *Will everything work out? Will I have alone time with God?* These feelings were intensified by the fact his adult son still lived at home. However, I was willing to give it all a chance.

Soon after settling in, the BDD manifested, when I started back to school. The time I spent in the bathroom increased, becoming more and more of a problem. It ultimately pushed me back into suicidal thinking once again. In addition, I felt smothered and dirty again being in this close and now immoral relationship. I buried myself in the compulsion of having to look "picture perfect" from the outside, because my insides became soiled again. I could not handle the guilt, condemnation, and shame building up inside of me. *I am living in sin. God forgive me.*

What a lie I was living! I was filled with the knowledge I was living in sin, while daring to think I was righteous. I realized God's grace and mercy no longer covered my nakedness, as I mistakenly stepped out of His presence and into a life of disobedience yet again. Had I cleaved t o His word, I would never have chosen the pitiable choice I made. At the time, I thought moving into Dave's home was a logical thing to do, yet it was far from the truth. How foolish and unwise one can become without truly seeking God for clear direction. I acted on my emotions, feelings, and fleshly desires instead of the inner leading of the Holy Spirit.

"There is a way that seems right to a man, but in the end it leads to destruction." —Proverbs 14:12 (NIV)

When I moved, I unintentionally departed from my harmonious carousel ride of stableness and catapulted back to the "wild roller coaster" I had previously escaped. The BDD ripped me apart while ghosts from my past resurfaced as I tried to live the new life I desperately desired. I did my best to hide and manage the awful turmoil hidden within me, yet as time evolved, it all oozed out from the crevasses of my mortal soul. No amount of makeup, hairspray, or fine clothing could cover up the confrontation I fought. I did my best on most days to retain the old smile I once truthfully wore. All I wanted was to be a good mom, a loving partner to Dave, and a kind individual to my family. *I am a counterfeit. I am not living the righteous life I should. I am a hypocrite.*

As each day passed, the unforeseen twists and turns from the "wild roller coaster" continued to unravel and fray my inner core. No amount of super glue could hold me together as I shattered into bits and pieces. Life became unbearable as I again craved death as a release from this misery. Guilt overwhelmed me. I desperately wanted to protect Dave the same way I often found myself protecting all my loved ones, my daughters, my mom, my siblings, and, yes, even my ex-husband. I did not want any of them involved in my craziness.

I mustered up the energy to live regardless of my distressing circumstances. Grooming and getting to school on time continued to be a huge problem. Often, I anxiously trembled from the bathroom, hoping to make it to school. Many times Dave coached me out of the bathroom in an attempt to get me out the door. He often drove me because I was in no condition to drive myself. The anxiety running through my entire body was excruciating and it was hard to get through classes with my mind fixated on thoughts of killing myself. I could no longer bear to uphold the fabricated life I projected out in the world. It felt like I was stitched together with threads that frayed and unraveled. *My God, My God, Why have I forsaken you? I am trapped in a valley of darkness with no end in sight. Why did I drift so far away from my sacred hiding place?*

Trying to make it to doctor appointments became unattainable. Dave drove me to these as well. With this inner whirlwind playing havoc with my life, I needed to lighten my course load at school once again. My doctor felt it was for the best, thinking school was too much for me while dealing with my latest breakdown. Battling to leave the house daily for school, the doctor's office, and other tasks, became unimaginably impossible—survival became the only thing I sought. I suffered a never-ending conflict between the obsessions in the mirror and my desire to continue living for my loved ones.

Thank God, I had occasional days of relief. Without them, I would never have made it. Ironically, most of my good days came when I needed them the most—usually when I spent time with Christina and Stephine. Christina was well aware of my condition, but Stephine had no idea how critical my situation was. After all, she lived with her dad and never witnessed me at my worst. I loved her visits, which always seemed to chase away my hideous mindset, allowing us to spend quality time together. We swam in the backyard pool, played tennis, and even went shopping, all without me being overly paranoid with my looks. I was a very different person whenever we were together. A strong, loving mom popped out as the ugly me stayed hidden within her coffin.

"I have discovered this principle of life— when I want to do what is right, I inevitably do what is wrong. I love God's law with all my heart. But there is another power within me that is at war in my mind. This power makes me a slave to the sin that is still within me. Oh, what a miserable person I am! Who will free me from this life that is dominated by sin? Thank God! The answer is in Jesus Christ our Lord." —Romans 7:21-25 (NIV)

Father God, I know I broke Your heart so many times because of unwise decisions. Had I consulted with You first and not make decisions based on feelings, I would not have suffered so much. I thank You for times of relief and bestowing me with good days to spend with my beloved daughters. Thank You so very much for your unconditional love even when I sin. Amen

---

- Have you ever made a major decision based on feelings?
- Do you consult with God on a regular basis regarding all your concerns, plans, and even good intentions?
- Do you recognize the harsh consequences that follow when you go astray and allow sin into your life?

Thirteen

Down she went…FAITH stepped in!

A year later, we discussed relocating to Florida. We both disliked the cold, winter months in Connecticut and mentally I did a little better during the warmer, sunnier days. We thought the move might help. Undoubtedly, this was a tougher decision on my part because I would be moving away from my daughters. Dave and I discussed the matter with my doctor and she felt it was a wise thing to consider. Her keen observations concerning my care lead her to believe that if I were away from the daily stresses and anxiety, I would have a better chance of recovery. Yet, she highly recommended I seek professional help if we decided to relocate. At this time, I grasped at whatever straws were available in order to stay alive. *What should I do? I need to escape this troublesome life.*

With my best interest at heart, my doctor advised me to fight through the OCD and BDD using behavioral therapy, assigning me simple challenges. One recommendation was to go out to eat with Dave once a week. Dave thought it was a great idea, but little did they understand it would propel me into the darkest, deepest crevices of my psyche. I tried to follow the doctor's advice, but fighting the images in the bathroom mirror caused me incredible despair. Even the simplest challenges daunted me. *I am getting worse. I am a prisoner in my own body. I want to be set free to be the real me!*

Many days and nights, I cried in Dave's arms like a little girl, beseeching him to help me get well so I could be a healthier mother. He assured me I would get well and I already was a wonderful mom. I truly did not want to die. All I desired was to be free from the torture chamber I lived in, within the mirror. Even worse, I pulled away from attending church. I knew it was wrong, but it was one less day I had to face the monster in the mirror. What I viewed as cowardice was a further drift away from God. I hid in the dark valley of doubt, afraid to face Him with my monstrous self. Yes, I still wrote in my prayer journal. Yes, I still read my Bible, but it felt like there was no connection. Perhaps I was wrongfully seeing Dave as a substitute for God, essentially an idol.

One day, unable to muster the words to explain to Dave what lived within me, I sat at my desk and drew pictures of all the thoughts occupying my mind. For hours on end, like a little child with a box of crayons and scribble pad, I drew one picture after another. Dave thought I was tending to my schoolwork, but instead I desperately unleashed the remnants of my past buried inside my mind. When I finished drawing my childish-looking pictures, I showed them to Dave. I explained, "This is a picture of my dad hanging on a tree. This is a picture of my house on fire. This is a picture of my step-dad's dead body with his boots melted to his feet. This is a picture of me held down and molested…" and the list went on. After showing Dave the entire collection, I tore them up and threw them into our fireplace. I hoped and prayed the flames would burn them up, setting me free from their oppression. I did not want to carry these ruins around with me anymore. I felt a slight degree of relief upon committing this ritualistic act, but it did not make enough of a difference.

The BDD became impossible. I was unable to get out of the house at all. I hoped if we relocated to Florida, maybe I would have a chance to reclaim my life. I was willing to grasp at any straw to avoid the anguish I was currently embroiled in, even if it meant moving away from my girls. I forced myself into believing everything would work out fine and my daughters could come to visit me whenever they wished. They both seemed to be fine with my decision. Thus, we decided to put the house on the market. The house sold within a few months. I trusted in God that this was His will as I continuously prayed to Him. Unbelievably, everything fell into place as I hoped. In hindsight, had I known the truth, I would not have made such a drastic change. Running away from my problems with the BDD was not the antidote.

At first, the relocation down to Florida went smoothly. The first few months went great, as Dave and I settled down in our new place. The BDD almost disappeared due to less involvement with others and the excitement over our new surroundings. However, it did not take very long for my negative train of thought to catch up with me. Yes, of course, the BDD reared its ugly head and thoughts of suicide crept in. The old baggage I hoped I left behind followed me. I suppose this is what they mean when one says, "a geographical location does not necessarily change your circumstances." Duh!

With thoughts of suicide mounting, I contemplated jumping off the Skyway Bridge: a cable stay bridge soaring high above the water into the endless sky. I fixated on the newspaper articles and television broadcasts reporting another jumper plummeted off the bridge into oblivion. How I wished it were I. I empathized with their wishes, for I longed to do the same. Dave never knew how close I'd come to plunging off it myself. During some walks around this enormous steel structure, I often plotted my own death. Each time the number of its victims increased, I wondered if I would be the next to make it onto the ever-growing list. Like a vulture keeping a keen watch out for its next meal, I kept my deliberation hidden until the appropriate time for me to take the defensible leap. It was just a matter of how many more terrible BDD attacks I would experience and how much more guilt, shame, and condemnation I could hold.

Yes, I lived in the beautiful, sunny state of Florida, yet I missed my children and I felt ashamed for leaving them behind. No longer was I able to look myself in the eye and say I was a good person. The guilt and shame mounting within me grew and I knew I needed to find a way back home so I could be back in my daughters' lives. On the other hand, I knew I had to do this on my own. I did not want Dave to relocate back with me. I felt too smothered by him. It felt like I never had an ounce of alone time to myself or with God. I felt bad feeling this way, yet something was not right and I had to figure a way out of the dire situation. I knew I did not want to hurt Dave's feelings, yet I needed to follow my heart. *This is not the time for me to be here. I have to get back home to my girls. Please God help me out!*

I spoke honestly to Dave about the guilt weighing on my heart. By no means was this easy. I loved him and did not want to lose him. After talking, we lovingly and equally decided I would relocate back to Connecticut by myself. We had no desire to end our relationship; we just needed to do what was best. I knew it would be a challenge for me to go back and try to make ends meet, yet I had this sense of peace within myself knowing God would provide for my needs. I was at wits end with life, yet for some reason I knew my only hope was in the Lord getting me back where I needed to be. Thank God, my faith in Him returned. I turned to the aid of several ministries I treasured.

"Rescue me from the mire, do not let me sink; deliver me from those who hate me, from the deep waters. Do not let the floodwaters engulf me or the depths swallow me up or the pit close its mouth over me.

Arise My Daughter

Answer me, O Lord, out of the goodness of your love; in your great mercy turn to me." —Psalm 69:14-16 (NIV)

Out of dire despair, I sent numerous prayer requests via the Internet advising the various ministries of my dilemma and my need to get back home unharmed. I knew I was under a spiritual attack and Satan wanted me dead, for the suicidal thinking running through my mind was at full throttle. However, I thank God I came to this realization because I was compelled to reach out to the ministries. As soon as I sent out all the prayer requests, immediately, I received the peace and calmness I craved. Instantaneously, I felt liberated and freed from the sinister thoughts lurking in my mind. Miraculously, God granted me the awesome power, strength, and ability to press onward in my journey to get back home, where He wanted me to be.

I embarked on a mission to find an apartment back home close to my daughters. I was not trying to escape from Dave. I just knew, beyond the shadow of a doubt, God wanted me all for himself so He could reestablish His healing process within me. I was one hundred percent confident that the perfect, affordable place would be waiting once I headed back to Connecticut to start searching. Dave and I decided to take a road trip there for a week to explore as many apartments as possible. As soon as we checked into our room, I sensed this task might be difficult to accomplish from a hotel, yet abundant faith assured me all would go well. I trusted in God, stepped out in faith, and began the search for the perfect apartment.

Sure enough, God did provide. I knew the place I found was a blessing from Him because every fine detail regarding the new rental fell perfectly into place. The apartment location granted me the blessed ability to live directly between both of my daughters, each only a few miles down the road. Once I signed all the paperwork with the property owner, Dave and I headed back to Florida so I could pack my belongings. During the ride, I felt as though I was in "la-la-land." I thanked God for placing such a wonderful and understanding man into my life. I knew that the distance between us would be hard for him to deal with, yet he knew I needed to do this in order to fulfill the desires of my broken heart. Dave knew I needed to get back to my daughters so I could be the best mother to them. He also knew I was still struggling with the BDD and thought the separation might help me deal with the issues plaguing my soul.

The "wild roller coaster" was too much for me to handle and I longed to escape before it took another wicked turn. I knew God had taken control. The peace and calmness bestowed upon me was a blessing that could only come from the joy of the Lord. In my heart, I knew I was on the right path again and I looked forward to my return trip home. It felt good knowing I was making the right decision.

"If any of you lacks wisdom, he should ask God, who gives generously to all without finding fault, and it will be given to him."
—James 1:5 (NIV)

It is amazing as I look back on all this and realize how sneaky and deceitful Satan is in leading people to believe certain choices we make are blessings from God. In my case, I thought relocating to Florida was the Lord's choice because everything that needed to take place fell rightly into place. First, my doctor advised the move, then the house sold at the same time Dave and I found a place in Florida. I had been misled into following what appeared to be a proper resolution at the time. At least I only spent several months in Florida before being directed back to where I belonged.

Father God, You are so good to those who seek to turn from their wrongdoing and place their hope in You. I praise You for snatching me out of the hands of the evil one as soon as I took a step of faith in reaching out to Your ministries. Surely, Your Spirit guided me to them. Thank You for making a way for me to return right back to where You wanted me to be. In Jesus' name, Amen

- Do you believe you are exactly where God wants you to be, or are you traveling in the wrong direction?
- Have you been thinking about running away from your problems instead of dealing with the issues at hand?
- Do you realize that there is a "perfect" time and season for certain things to take place in your life?

Fourteen

Journey Back Home

The journey back to Connecticut went smoothly in spite of the feelings Dave and I experienced when separating—two hearts torn apart with so much distance between us. However, we knew it was for the best and assured each other it would be only temporary. I settled down into my private place of refuge before the holidays. No longer living in sin and under condemnation was a huge relief—a breathtaking sanction. What a joy and honor to cook a scrumptious Thanksgiving meal in my tidy safe haven. It was a double blessing sharing it with my loved ones without having any onslaughts in the bathroom. Not only did I reap the rewards of relocating in time for the holidays, I also enjoyed celebrating my youngest daughter Stephine's sixteenth birthday, which falls between Thanksgiving and Christmas. I considered this continuous harmony a gift from God. No amount of money in the world could buy the love, joy, and peace given me during this heart-touching time, being back in my daughters' lives and under the watchful eye of my Creator.

"Humble yourselves before the Lord, and he will lift you up."
—James 4:10 (NIV)

The forlorn separation between Dave and I continued. However, I remained grateful, steadfast, and in high spirits, knowing God directed my journey back. I counted the separation as a blessing for Dave. The distance between us protected him from the despair I imposed upon him during my out of control BDD attacks and their unspeakable ramifications. I knew God was protecting him from additional harm as I continuously prayed to Him to protect all my beloved ones from the panic-stricken mindset I frequently fell captive to. Fortunately, the BDD went into dormancy when I relocated and resided alone. By the grace of God, the upturn from the hopeless situation in Florida allowed me the ability to gain a better frame of mind. I continued to make the best of my circumstances and took the good days along with a few bad ones.

I decided to go back to school in hopes of finishing my degree in accounting. With only four classes remaining, I opted to start with one. I knew I needed to do something to advance myself and to challenge the low self-image I carried. I decided to persevere, trusting in God to assist me in pushing through my fear and futile ways of living. I knew in my heart that I was not living life to its fullest. Being shut-in, tucked away, and hidden from society was not going to happen. I longed to become a functioning, productive part of everyday life. However, had I known what lurked ahead, I would not have attempted to do such a thing, yet.

All hell broke loose the first day of class. I planned to shower and groom several hours prior to leaving for school, as I did not want to be late. As I groomed the BDD manifested and again forced havoc within my soul. Hour, after hour, trapped in a grueling grooming ritual, seeing unsightly images appearing in the mirror and listening to the lies bombarding my mind. *You are ugly. I would rather be dead than be plagued with this.* I could not make myself look "good enough" to go out in public. Trapped in the midst of my biggest fear, it took every ounce of energy to force myself out of my apartment and to school.

The anxiety thrashed through my body as I drove, besieging me. I swerved in and out of traffic, and with every honk from passing vehicles, my heart pounded even more. As I shook out of control, the steering wheel felt like a jackhammer set on high. I could not believe I was driving under such extreme panic. My mind and thoughts were nowhere on the road, but instead trapped in dreadful lies about my life, future, and thoughts of suicide.

As I approached the school, thoughts of driving to the top of the high-rise parking garage and jumping off overcame me. Ensnared in a state of obscurity, I drove to the highest level of the parking garage filled with the repulsive thought of killing myself. I despised struggling in the bathroom over my looks and detested going out in public afterwards. Fortunately, God prohibited me from following through with my plans. As I turned my thoughts toward Him, a glimmer of hope rescued me from this ruinous path—just in the knick of time. I quickly turned around and drove to the lower level.

After safely parking, I proceeded into the school in an attempt to attend my first day of class. As I hurried through the corridors that appeared to be a constricting tunnel, anxiety and fear suffocated me. Immediately I made my way into the nearest bathroom hoping to regain my composure before class started. As soon as I stepped into the bathroom, I locked myself in one of the stalls trying to hide my agony from everyone. I did not want anyone to witness me in this condition. As I trembled in the locked stall, I visualized pounding my head into the large wall-mounted mirrors, hoping to divert my mind from its evil, illogical thoughts. *I am too ugly to be out in public. I will always remain captive to this disorder. I will never live a normal life.* I did my best to calm down as I proceeded out of the stall and cautiously headed to class. The only thing on my mind was to find a seat in the back, pull out a sheet of paper, and start writing my deadening feelings to God. Whenever I was filled with great grief and despair, this technique helped a great deal. It calmed me down enough to take my mind off the daunting thoughts.

When class ended, I rushed to my car in hopes of making it home safely. As I made my way into the car, gushing waves of tears washed over me. How I ever found the ignition and positioned the key, I truly do not know. All the way home I bawled hysterically and prayed to God to protect me.

Once home, I called Dave to inform him of the discouraging occurrence. Out of anguish, I expressed what took place and told him I would be unable to continue the class. Greatly concerned, he agreed with my resolution. I knew if I experienced another alarming day like the first, most likely I would be found dead. So once again, I withdrew from class and school altogether. Thus, as usual, I went into hibernation asking God to restore and strengthen me.

After several weeks of restoration, I received a call from one of my brothers asking if I would like to do some light accounting work from his home. I counted the call a blessing, an immediate answer to my prayers as my income remained limited and I needed additional earnings to make ends meet. Held captive to the curtailing BDD by no means allowed me the freedom to work a regular job, thus I continued collecting Social Security Disability. I graciously accepted his proposal. I loved working with figures and knew my previous recordkeeping skills would be useful. The opportunity allowed me to find the courage to press past my fear and the distorted body image that I perceived to be real, even though it was only to his house.

I am not certain whether he had any substantial knowledge of the disturbing disorder I fought at the time. We never had much of a relationship. For the most part, he kept his life private. Often, I'd ask myself, "Who is he?" I kept asking this question, as I became a part of his life.

Whenever in his presence, I felt as though I was an ungodly person and he was a saint. He always walked around with a big smile on his face praising the Lord. However, I began to sense what was taking place, behind his facade. I sensed something was not right. I soon realized he was hiding behind the same make-believe masks I held–trying to pretend all is well, with our phony "plastered smiles" on our faces, in an attempt to hide the turmoil brewing within.

I never realized how much of God's Word and Spirit I held. I suppose that is why I discerned that something was not right in my brother's life. The burden placed upon me to pray on his behalf day and night, was enormous. I never experienced the weight of such a burden—praying for someone else. It forced me to take my mind off my own circumstances and turn my entire attention to someone else. I still fought the BDD in the bathroom every time I went to his house. However, I was willing to battle with it because I knew it was my mission to help someone else.

The light broke through as I realized what was taking place. Not only was I helping my brother, but I was also deepening my devotional time with the Lord. I knew I was still in a spiritual battle. Therefore, I kept listening and watching sermons via radio and TV, kept reading my Bible, and continued to pray—the defense I needed to win. I longed to be free from the affliction destroying me for over sixteen years. I knew doctors and medicine were not going to fix my problem. Only the Lord could heal and rescue me from the enemy's camp. Even though I felt tired and defeated most of the time, I still did my best to keep moving forward. I knew God had greater plans to use me.

However, after months of holding up under the unbearable task, I had no choice but to detach from my brother's life. He was dabbling in an area of weakness that I did not want to be associated with. At this time, he was caught in his own spiritual battle and I was not equipped to ransom him. From my own experiences, I knew only God could rescue him from the enemy's camp. I felt terrible pulling away, but there was no doubt that God was directing me to do it. Out of love and concern, I told him he was not well and needed help.

Politely, I informed him I was going to take a step back while he did what he needed to do to get back on track.

"For I know the plans I have for you, declares the Lord, plans to prosper you and not to harm you, plans to give you hope and a future." —Jeremiah 29:11

Abba, Whenever I humble myself before You, You lift my soul from despair to hope. Thank You for saving me from the enemies' camp and placing my feet on a better path. If I had not placed my hope in You, I would have missed the opportunity to serve You by helping my brother in his time of need. I thank You, Lord, for the wonderful plans You have for me and all who trust in You. In Jesus' name, Amen

---

- Have you been hiding behind a "phony mask" trying to cover-up your inner turmoil? If so, have you spoken to at least one other person regarding your "inner" struggle?
- Do you know that God has a wonderful plan for your future?
- Are you in the habit of journaling on a regular basis?

"Let the morning bring me word of your unfailing love, for I have put my trust in you. Show me the way I should go, for to you I lift up my soul."

—Psalm 143:8 (NIV)

Fifteen

Wisdom to Disconnect

"But the wisdom that comes from heaven is first and all pure; then peace-loving, considerate, submissive, full of mercy and good fruit, impartial and sincere." —James 3:17 (NIV)

Breaking away from all interaction with my brother allowed me the opportunity to spend the summer months with my daughter Stephine. The school year was over and she was looking forward to working a summer job with me. My previous employer agreed to let her work the part-time, seasonal pool job I worked for him in the past. Stephine was not old enough to work the job alone due to age regulations, but if I accompanied her, it was okay. Psychologically, I was not strong enough to be working, yet I was willing to endure the distress in order to build my relationship with her. I enjoyed having the opportunity to assist her at the job in spite of my insecurities. Working the seasonal position allowed Stephine to gain work experience, which led her to a new job opportunity of her own.

I fully acknowledged God was orchestrating my life as He provided Stephine with her first real job—located directly below my apartment. I enjoyed bringing her an evening meal whenever she desired and to chitchat with her about school and boys. This may sound silly, but for me it was a tremendous opportunity to be a part of her life. To assist and witness Stephine obtain her driver's license, finding her first job, and seeing her dolled up for her junior prom were divine blessings. I never imagined I would be alive to watch it all take place. So many special opportunities such as these occurred, confirming I was right where God wanted me to be.

After a few months, my brother called and asked for my assistance again. He was anxious to have me back and assured me he was doing well. I will admit, at first I was very apprehensive because I had lost trust in him, yet I wanted to help him once again. Another concern was my ability to creep around the unease in the mirror and being out in public. I hid my apprehension from him. I did not want to concern him with my discomfort, because he desperately needed me back.

While giving him a second chance, I formed a special bond with his children. While spending time with the two of them, they taught me a great deal about Jesus. Innocently, they deposited their childlike faith into my heart, deepening my own relationship with Christ. I never imagined two young children would be teaching me. The biggest gift they passed on to me was their belief and understanding of Christmas.

One day, while sitting at the kitchen table with them, one showed me a picture he had drawn. It was a picture of baby Jesus resting in a manger and he wrote "Happy Birthday Jesus" above it. They professed they were celebrating Jesus' birthday as Christmas approached. This revealing occurrence illuminated my ignorance of the true meaning of Christmas, and became the catalyst for me to write and publish a children's picture book called, *The True Meaning of Christmas, The Greatest Gift of All.*

My heart wept over all the lost years I raised my daughters and placed a manger under our tree without any understanding of what I was doing. I thought of it as just another Christmas decoration. No one ever explained what it represented. All I ever heard and saw featured Santa, bundles of presents, and Oh! I need not leave out "Happy Holidays" chanted all over the place. How ignorant I was about so many things. As the saying goes, better late than never. However, I wish I had learned this at an earlier age rather than my early thirties.

As mentioned before, I attended church as a child, but my mind was closed. None of it penetrated my heart until I was saved—when I acknowledged and accepted Jesus Christ into my heart and life. It was at this point I learned the true celebration of Easter. Then two blessed children taught me the true meaning of Christmas. *What coffin had I been living in? Thank God, my casket finally opened.*

"If the Good News we preach is hidden behind a veil, it is hidden only from people who are perishing. Satan, who is the god of this world, has blinded the minds of those who don't believe. They are unable to see the glorious light of the Good News. They don't understand this message about the glory of Christ, who is the exact likeness of God."
—2 Corinthians 4: 3-4 (NLV)

As months passed, my brother lost his footing again. It was tough going to his house knowing he was on the wrong road leading away from God. I tried to confront him about the issue, but he continued to deny my accusations. I hung in as long as I could while he descended downwards. It seemed as if I was in the middle of a hurricane, yet it was not my own storm. Finally, I came to my senses and acknowledged his problem was out of my control and I stepped far away from the situation. Thankfully, a few weeks later he awakened to his transgression and sought help.

Father God, I praise You for wisdom that comes from Heaven that allows me to make wise decisions here on earth when reaching out to aid others. I am ever so grateful for all You have done in allowing my daughter, Stephine, and I to experience special moments together. I praise You for opening up the eyes of my heart so that two blessed, little children could deposit more of Your "Good News" into my mind regarding the true meaning of Christmas. Thank You for working a miracle in my brother's life as well. In Jesus' name, Amen

- Do you need to give someone a second chance?
- Have you ever stopped to notice how God strategically works things out in your life while you reach out to help others?
- Do you clearly understand the true essence of Christmas and Easter?

"In prayer there is a connection between what God does and what you do. You can't get forgiveness from God, for instance, without also forgiving others. If you refuse to do your part, you cut yourself off from God's part."

—Mathew 6:14 (TM)

Chapter Sixteen

The Opening of Pandora's Box

When I pulled away from my brother's transgression, I realized how seriously impaired most of my siblings were. The addictions plaguing my entire family via drugs, alcohol, or mental illness became more apparent to me, as I fought to maintain my own recovery. My eyes opened to the truth of the tribulations manifesting through my lineage. No wonder I kept trying to run away from it all. It was pure ill will and I just did not know how to accept it. My sister, Debby, often told me to love the sinner, yet hate the sin. However, I began to struggle in agreeing with this saying. I knew it was time to take a stand and declare that I could no longer deny that my family was flooded with addictions, mental illness, and generational curses. To make matters worse, the disgrace had already seeped down to the next generation. *What will it take to break this generational curse of abuse and darkness?*

No sooner had I detached from my brother's affairs than I received a call from my younger sister Kim. She wanted to know if I would hook up with her and have some sister time. It broke my heart when I told her "no." I no longer was going to accept or pretend her self-destructive abuse was not a problem. I told her she was just as sick as the rest of the family. I suggested she seek professional help, because I was not well enough to deal with her or anyone else's addictions and self-destructive ways anymore. I had it! The adversity playing havoc throughout my family had nearly destroyed me. It was awful witnessing the adversity that was infecting my family and, as a result, I became sick. My weight dropped to a mere 97 pounds—forcing me to seek professional help, again!

At this critical point, I headed to my primary care doctor for help. I needed something to calm my nerves and figured she would prescribe some sort of aid. As I explained my insufferable condition to her, she quickly acknowledged the distressing state I held. She prescribed a medication, hoping to ease my fraying nerves. Upon leaving, I realized how shattered I was. The historic plague weaving through my kin was extremely bad, and I was thoroughly entangled in it. In fact, it was so bad, I nearly lost sight of the horrify BDD destroying my life.

Leaving her office, I rapidly drove to the nearest pharmacy to fill the new prescription, believing it would quiet my nerves. As soon as I got home, I forced open the bottle and popped the pill into my mouth, swallowing it as quickly as possible. As I ingested it, I realized this was not the solution to my dilemma. One minute, I wallowed in dire need, desperate to take the pill, and the next second I could not wait for the medicine to leave my body. A small voice within, God's Holy Spirit, assured me I did not need to take the pills. I would be doing myself more harm than good. At this cross road, I knew God was still with me and I was going to make it through this adversity no matter how bad things looked at the time.

I felt glad deciding not to take anymore of the medication. I knew the answer to my problems was not in a bottle—God was my source, my healer. It was something I had known all along, yet I kept stumbling back into my old patterns and into the hands of my adversary. I truly believed more and more that the only way out of my struggle was through my faith in God. By this time, I was worn-out from all the difficulties I experienced and kept praying to God for guidance.

One day, I stumbled across an ad in the newspaper looking for volunteers to participate in a study at Yale New Haven Psychiatric Hospital. They were conducting experimental treatment options for people suffering with conditions similar to mine. I immediately wanted to participate in hopes of being able to prevent others from suffering as much as I suffered. This objective propelled me. I phoned them and after a short interview, scheduled an appointment to meet with them.

Our first meeting was intense as I related a great deal of my past to them. The doctor conducting the interview was very nice. I enjoyed her sincere concern for my overall wellbeing. She did a wonderful job in retrieving information. When the meeting ended, she assured me that she would be getting back to me within a few days. Sure enough, she called to tell me they needed additional information in order to proceed. She also informed me of something I did not know. After going through my data, they believed I was suffering from yet another condition called Post Traumatic Stress Syndrome. She emphasized that when my great-grandmother died my life had abruptly shifted. Evidently, I did not process the situation in a healthy way. When she relayed this information to me, I felt a burden lift. I thanked her for the insight and assured her I would see her and the rest of the staff soon.

"Then you will know the truth, and the truth will set you free."
— John 8:32 (NIV)

After digesting her information, memories from my past invaded my mind, and my heart. Feelings from my great-grandmother Mary's death surfaced. Emotions stuffed deep down inside stirred up. Sixteen years had passed since her death and I wept in a way I had never grieved before. Yes, I cried dreadfully at her funeral, but a few days later the tears stopped so I could press on in life. As tears streamed down my face now and my heart began to let go of the pain, I sensed a heartwarming comfort within my soul. I finally succumbed to the deep mourning of her death. I accepted the fact she was resting in peace and if she received Jesus Christ into her heart, I would be seeing her again.

The second interview was even more intense than the first. Dave came up from Florida to visit me for a few days, and they allowed him to be present during parts of the interview. With him attending the interview, he became more aware of the pain I lived with. He knew I was not well, yet he never fully grasped how serious my inner turmoil was. He always remained hopeful that I would get better when I escaped the adversity around me. He did not understand what I meant when I told him it was the inside stuff and not the outside things that were killing me. For this reason, I wanted him to sit through most of the consultation so he could observe what I needed to expose–the guilt, pain, and the unbearable remorse I kept trying to hide or cleanup.

The doctors questioned numerous times, as to whether I would be willing to go on medication. They felt it would definitely help in terms of improving the quality of my life. They told Dave there were many new medications and I should consider giving the new ones a chance. They knew I was not in favor of going on medications because of my history. Adamantly, I refused. I knew if I started medication again thoughts of suicide would inevitably evolve. I was not willing to take the risk again. Even though I declined going on medication, they still desired my participation in their study.

Part of the procedure involved me taking home a packet of questionnaires. I filled them out honestly, and to the best of my ability. They addressed my past and present circumstances. It took several hours to complete all the questions and after doing so, I finally realized what I had gone through. It blew my mind when I outlined and then penned all the dreary details. It opened my eyes to the fact I had come a long way and was still alive for a reason. I had never taken time to reflect back on my life. Filling out the questionnaires forced me to look at the historical darkness. However, after reading the requirements of participation in the study, I decided not to partake. I did not want to put my body through the nerve-racking tests required, nor did I want to ingest the substances required.

To sum it up, I called the doctors back and advised them of my decision not to participate. They were understanding and extended their services to me regardless. Even though I was unable to assist them in their study, they were still very concerned for my well-being and willing to continue my treatment. I knew these doctors were the best in this field, yet I also knew; deep down, this was not the path for me. I told them it was kind of them to extend their services and I would phone them if I decided to take them up on their offer.

After the layer of grief from my great-grandmother's death peeled away, additional layers of repressed memories surfaced. One day while going through my grooming ritual, images from my childhood appeared in my mirror. The appalling visions sickened me. I dropped to the bathroom floor while tears and disbelief overwhelmed me.

I remembered being sexually molested. However, it was at a much earlier age than I previously recalled. I was just a little girl, eight years old at the time. I wondered why I had not remembered these things earlier. My sister always told me God reveals a little at a time because if He revealed all the sorrow at once, I would not be able to handle it. I suppose He thought that if I was strong enough to handle the grief of my great-grandmother's death the truth of being molested at an earlier age could be handled too.

Now, more anxious than before, I did not know what the next step was for my recovery. I felt trapped not knowing what to do or expect. I felt stuck in life. At this pivotal point, after viewing my life and my family's history, I felt a tugging in my heart to write a book.

My heart fluttered like a butterfly, thinking about the idea as I sensed great hopes of healing and vision of being set free to help others.

"For the Son of Man came to find and restore the lost."
—Luke 19:10 (TM)

Dear Lord, At times truth is hard to digest and accept, but truth is what sets captives free. Thank You for opening the eyes of my heart to truth and for being with me as Your Spirit peeled away the hurtful layers that needed tending and mending. I praise You for planting a seed of hope and a vision to heal within my heart. My "desire" is to write with a pure heart bent towards reaching out to those who are hurting...wrapped in the wounds of their past and perhaps even on the verge of ending their lives. May my transparency and willingness to share Your miraculous love for all humanity be turned into a widespread ministry of healing. To You be all the glory, honor, and praise. In Jesus' name, Amen

---

- Have you ever taken time out to reflect upon your past?
- If you have been wounded and are still hurting, are you ready to allow God to reveal, tear away, and remove the old ruins from your past?
- Are you ready to allow God's Holy Spirit to heal and restore you from the inside out?

"Search me, O God, and know my heart; test me and know my anxious thoughts."

—Psalm 139:23 (NIV)

Seventeen

Vision to Heal

"Where there is no vision, the people perish."
—Proverbs 29:18 (KJV)

Numerous times, I told Dave I wanted to write a book about my disabling condition. He responded positively, encouraging me to follow through with my good intentions. I pondered the idea for a long drawn-out time. I never took action because it required re-examining many painful years. I did not want to relive the horrible times. However, this time I was unable to flee from this dream—the writing of this book. I never imagined I had the qualifications it took, because my writing, spelling, and grammar were by no means up to par. Faith allowed me to envision this book in its entirety: as long as I did my part, God would step in and provide the rest. I knew within my heart that it was my mission and purpose for still being alive.

As I plotted the outline, a vibrant sensation stirred within, confirming that God was calling me to take on this assignment. While working on the first few chapters words came effortlessly without much thought. I had no idea where all the information came from. It was as if a completely different person took over. Each time I finished an episode, I pulled away more relieved and empowered. I knew it was imperative to my survival to carry out this mission. I also acknowledged this book would aid other hurting souls, especially women.

Even though I was not where I wanted to be regarding my healing, I pressed on. Trapped and isolated from society, I was able to work on this book. Some days went great and other days I could not bring myself to work on it. On these days, despair had the best of me, locking my mind on my disabling condition. My warped thinking constantly distracted me—thoughts of never overcoming the BDD and living a normal life. At times, I nearly collapsed under the unfathomable distractions, lies, and ugly distortions, yet by the grace of God, I would tune into sermons, helping me trudge through the valley of darkness. Truly, I was in a spiritual battle and my defense was to continue praying and pressing on in faith. *If I finish this book, I will be unleashed as the woman God destined me to be. My prison gate will open. The shackles will be broken. I will be set free to live.* I kept reminding myself.

As mentioned before, I was not doing well dealing with all the heartbreaking things taking place. My brother with his unfortunate circumstances, my sister with her tribulations, and the continuous upheaval from the rest of my family was oppressive. With this confrontation taking place, I knew I needed a break from everything and everyone. I decided to visit Dave in Florida for a few weeks, hoping to recuperate and clear my mind. I was also anxious to share with him the first several chapters of the book I had completed. I knew I was onto something big.

Sad to say, the trip did not turn out as I hoped. A few days into the visit, I received a distressing phone call from my daughter, Christina. She informed me that my younger sister, Kim, had died. She was only thirty-six years old. Her lifeless body was found in the back seat of her car by a few of her so-called friends. She too was trying to escape from her horrible past and attempted suicide several times. I was sad when I received the news because I wished to share this book with her, hoping it might help her deal with her own childhood memories, and frequent battles with suicide.

At this time, my mind was so wilted there was no way I would make it back to Connecticut for the funeral. I knew the BDD would be unbearable while getting ready for the funeral. I would be setting myself up for my own suicide. *If I do not make it to the funeral because of the BDD, they will be burying me next.* The thought of facing those battles again frightened me. I thank God I was away when she died. It shielded me from additional heartache.

A week after the funeral, I returned to Connecticut. Traveling back and forth trying to keep a bond with Dave in Florida and my two daughters in Connecticut played havoc on my life. I despised traveling because of the BDD. It continuously tore me to pieces. In spite of the grave circumstances, I firmly pressed on writing this book, now with a stronger purpose due to my sister's death.

Once I retreated to my safe hiding place back in Connecticut, I realized how serious my condition was. I feared going out in public and could not imagine taking part in anything requiring me to groom before it. This became more apparent when Dave flew out to California to attend his daughter's wedding. I chose not to go because

I knew I was not well enough to attend such an affair. I remained captive to the hideous distortions in the mirror, the grueling grooming rituals that kept me locked up. I longed to live a normal life like everyone else, and being trapped caused a great deal of misery, I desperately desired to end my life again. The only bright spot that helped me through this dark time were the phone calls I received from my daughters, and the little things I did with them. This allowed me to hang on and hang in there in hopes of better days to come.

Regardless of my circumstance, I felt better whenever I worked on this book. Unbelievably, I became more and more grateful for all the pain and suffering I had gone through. I recognized it was all part of God's plan to change me from what I was to who I am today. The best part of getting better was the fact that my mind became clearer, allowing me to see the actual goodness of God's hands at work in my life. Little by little, God's Holy Spirit was transforming me from within. My heart, mind, conduct, and speech were being renewed through this reconstruction project. I had faith that God was diligently changing me from the inside out. It was as if I lived life the opposite of how God wanted me to live.

As I continued to pour my heart into this book, more and more despair and gloom fled from me. As God gently pealed each layer away, I wept over the acknowledgments. Coming to terms with my past and handing the sorrow over to God brightened up my days. Being cleansed, and refreshed, I began to see a lovely person in the mirror. It was perfect timing with the holidays just around the corner.

With Thanksgiving Day approaching, I set out to have a wonderful dinner by inviting my daughters, Christina and Stephine, as well as my ex-husband. I included Rob because I did not want him to be alone. Even though we were divorced for over ten years, we maintained a respectable friendship, never belittling one another like stereotypical divorced couples. This allowed us the privilege to raise our daughter, Stephine, without confrontation. We wanted the best for her and it was imperative we respect one another. Dave did not have a problem with Rob coming. He understood my desire to reach out to others.

When Thanksgiving morning arrived, I joyfully seasoned the turkey and placed it in the oven to cook. As time passed, I prepared the rest of the meal, visualizing the lovely time awaiting us. What made it even more serene? I did not incur any onslaughts in the bathroom. I remained relaxed and present for the joyful event. However, Thanksgiving did not go the way I planned. Christina decided to go to her boyfriend's house and Stephine worked later than she expected. However, Rob came. We savored the delicious meal and had a wonderful conversation regarding the girls.

Just when I thought the day was over, the telephone rang. To my surprise, it was Stephine crying and upset over her long, exhausting workday. It was a blessing to be able to comfort her with loving words of encouragement. She asked for a warm dish of leftovers to be brought over. Even though I was in my pajamas, settled under a cozy blanket, I rose to the opportunity to tend to her aid. It gave me great pleasure to prepare a warm Thanksgiving meal, a few desserts, and a hand-written note tucked in between telling her I loved her.

The days following Thanksgiving were blessed ones as well. Stephine stopped over to enjoy additional leftovers, giving us the opportunity to chat. I counted little occasions like these as gifts from God. They always arrived when I needed them the most. Each time I lost hope with my disabling condition, one of my daughters miraculously phoned, brightening up my day. I pleaded with God to heal me from the BDD. I pleaded so I could be a decent mother. However, the BDD lingered as though it was a thorn in my flesh.

"To keep me from becoming conceited because of these surpassingly great revelations, there was given me a thorn in my flesh, a messenger from Satan, to torment me. Three times I pleaded with the Lord to take it away from me. But he said to me, 'My grace is sufficient for you, for my power is made perfect in weakness.' Therefore, I will boast all the more gladly about my weaknesses, so that Christ's power may rest on me." —2 Corinthians 12:7-9

Shortly after Thanksgiving, I fell back into despair over the BDD and became suicidal again. My thoughts were atrocious and I longed for a drink, hoping to drown the dreadful reflections. However, by the grace of God, I surmounted the temptation, which was a deadly trap leading to destruction. Obviously, the 'wild roller coaster' I had been on was still in full throttle. However, I knew in my heart, God was going to make good use of me. I believed! The good works He started within were part of His master plan to turn my life around.

Stephine's eighteenth birthday approached and I was thankful to be alive. We enjoyed a marvelous day of celebration. She had no idea how important things like this were to me as I continued to hide my woes from her. I never had the chance to build a strong relationship with her because of my illness, but I continued to work at it. I knew from my own prior feelings toward my mother that some things come in time.

During my younger years, I disliked my mother. I secretly hid this hatred deep within my heart and I did not fully recognize it. In fact, it was at the onset of writing this book that I began to see and realize what my mother went through. With this knowledge, I turned to God and asked for His forgiveness for the hatred I had in my heart toward my mother and everyone else I despised. This change of heart emphasized that God's Holy Spirit was doing awesome things within me as I grew in His love.

The thought of never overcoming the BDD often forced me to lose all hope. I called Dave in Florida many times and told him I could not handle life. I informed him it was impossible for me to settle back in Florida with him. I could not live with myself trapped in fear, anxiety, and low self-esteem. How could anyone else deal with me! Regardless of my woes, he remained peaceful, willing to put up with my highs and dreadful lows because he had seen the love and goodness inside of me. He knew the other part of me, the awful side, was not the real me. He continuously reassured me everything would improve.

Unfortunately, one evil night, I hit rock bottom yet again. The torture in the bathroom wasted several excruciating hours of ridiculous obsessive grooming without purpose. *Come on Barb. Give it up! You're only going to sleep.* Filled with fear, anxiety, and exhaustion, I crawled into bed with my prayer journal and begged God to take me home so I could be with Him. I extended farewell writings to my beloved ones, expressing my last wishes of love to all of them. As I rested my head on my Bible, I cried myself to sleep. The following morning, when I awoke, I went into deep prayer with God, asking for help. The infinite peace I held, the warmth that encompassed me assured me He had me in the palm of his hands.

"You turned my wailing into dancing; you removed my sackcloth and clothed me with joy, that my heart may sing to you and not be silent. O Lord my God, I will give you thanks forever."
—Psalm 30:11-12 (NIV)

Thank goodness, God rescued me! Christmas was approaching and Dave wanted to visit. He missed me dearly and worried over all I was suffering. I knew the visit would be a challenge, not knowing what to expect with the troublesome BDD. Yet, I had faith that all would go well. Thanks be to God everything worked out wonderfully. Dave, my daughters and I had a magnificent Christmas as my annoying disorder went dormant for a while.

Dear Lord, I am so thankful for Your Spirit imparting within me the vision to heal so that I would not perish amid the ruins of my past and present sufferings. I trust in time that You will completely remove the annoying "thorn in my flesh", but until then I know that Your grace is sufficient in my times of weakness. Thank You for well-needed episodes of remission from my archenemy, the BDD, granting me freedom and peace to enjoy my beloved ones' company. In Jesus' name, Amen

---

- Has God placed a blessed vision within your heart?
- Have you been working with God in seeing that dream become a reality?
- Are you currently holding any grudges or resentment towards your mother and/or father? If so, have you ever considered what they may have gone through or tried to "hide" while doing their best to raise you?

Eighteen

More Truths & Blessings

After Dave returned to Florida, I became extremely ill—nauseous, fatigued, and plagued with unbearable joint pain. I believed the endless stress from the BDD created this sickness. My body ached from head to toe, as though a train had run over me a dozen times. Acid brewed in my stomach, producing a painful burning sensation. I ate a well-balanced diet and exercised daily, but it did not matter. My body continued to deteriorate. With my health declining, I visited my primary care physician. The physical examination and blood work showed nothing out of the norm. Therefore, she referred me to a specialist for my stomach problem.

The earliest available appointment was two weeks away. The waiting was grueling, I felt worse with each passing day. I eliminated certain foods from my diet, yet nothing freed me from the stomach distress. In an effort to keep my stress level down, I avoided grooming as much as possible. I did not need extra toxins invading my body. Just the thought of grooming caused the burning sensation in my stomach to intensify. Inundated with pain, I decreased my daily exercise as well.

My appointment with the specialist finally arrived. She immediately scheduled me for an upper and lower endoscopy. The procedures required that I fast three days before the internal examination of my stomach and colon. Fasting did not bother me; I hoped it might even help. I knew believers in Christ fast during times of need, and for clarity and deeper union with God. Thus, as I prepared to fast, I prayed and asked God to shed light on my problems, because I could not live this way anymore. I was at the end of my rope, yet again.

During the first day of fasting and seeking God, I became conscious of my preoccupation with food, exercise, and even the bathroom scale. Everyday my mind focused on what, when, and how much I was going to eat and exercise. I never realized my life revolved around these things. From the time I awoke to the time I went to bed, my thoughts centered on food, exercise, and the number on the scale. Every meal precisely planned as well as the dire need to exercise in the morning and evening. It took fasting and prayer along with a serious bout of illness to make me face the truth—the majority of my thoughts and life gyrated around these fixations. Moreover, it took an awesome God to allow me to face the reality.

Upon completing the three-day fast and undergoing the examinations, I was happy and relieved that the test results did not show anything major wrong. However, the doctor thought I had irritable bowel syndrome and prescribed a medication to help remedy the discomfort. Unfortunately, it did very little to help my stomach, fatigue, or body aches. However, I continued to pray to God, asking Him to heal and guide me through this bout of illness.

I spent most of my days indoors, because of the cold winter months, and devoted my attention to writing this book. I knew God had called me to write my life's journey. I also knew He wanted me to surrender my fixations toward food, exercise, and the bathroom scale. Working on the book was no problem as I learned more truths about God and myself. Yet, I knew it would still be a challenge to overcome my neurotic control of the other three—food, exercise and the dreadful scale. However, I did not want these "things" to be the core of my life anymore, because I knew Christ was to be the center. Thank God for revelations!

Shortly after acknowledging the truths, I threw my bathroom scale out. As I carried it out of my apartment, I wore a broad smile. I knew I was making a wise move and was headed in the proper direction towards healing and freedom. I flung it into the dumpster with a huge sigh of relief. When I hurled the all-consuming thing into the trash, a huge weight lifted from my shoulders, I had been liberated. *I am free. You will not control my life anymore.* I rushed back to my apartment to give Dave a call. I wanted to share the great news with him. Filled with excitement, I told him. He was pleased because he knew how addicted and out of control I was. I had never realized I would become a slave to a piece of metal with numbers on it.

For a few days, I felt lost without the scale. It played a vital role in my life. I desperately wanted to buy a new one but I overcame the urge. I wanted to win this battle and I knew I would not make progress if I bought another one.

Unfortunately, I slipped a few times. A store located down the street had a huge public scale. As soon as you walked into the store, it stared you right in the eye. No one entering or exiting the store could miss the doggone thing. I did most of my shopping there, and out of compulsion, I weighed myself on numerous occasions. However, as time passed, I overcame the desire. I realized that I allowed a stupid scale to dictate how I felt about myself. If my weight was up a pound or two, I was miserable. If it was below a certain number, I felt pleased. It took determination and the power of God's Holy Spirit working within, to make me realize my true worth is not based upon what number shows up on the scale. My true worth and happiness comes from within and knowing God—how He sees me, and what Christ accomplished on the cross on my behalf.

"So if the Son sets you free, you will be free indeed."
—John 8:36 (NIV)

On the other hand, my other two issues, food and exercise, were a more difficult battle. In fact, it took me a few years to put them in their proper place. I had so many hang-ups that needed undoing; the process took awhile to surrender. However, I remained grateful for the small victories taking place in my life and even the slip-ups, as I learned from them. I fully trusted that the Lord would eventually deliver me from them too.

Shut in and tucked away from society no longer bothered me as it did before. Each day I thanked God for giving me the time to read His word, watch sermons on television, and listen to the Christian radio station. Throughout the entire winter and spring, He had me in a cleansing process that was, in fact, therapeutic. Letting go of my childhood memories as I worked on this book and no longer being a slave to the scale helped immensely.

Once again, I began to like the person in the mirror. I knew I was being transformed and I enjoyed the person God was revealing. The masks, cover-ups, and plastered-on smiles were fading away again, as I continued to journey through the transformation process. This could not have occurred at a better time for it prepared me to step out of hiding and enjoy the beautiful summer. I was eager to embrace the new season of life, even though I still suffered major joint pain and occasional bouts of the BDD. I hoped in time it would all die away as my tainted inside continued in the healing and purification process-taking place.

As I stepped out of my shell, life blossomed. I was living life with a renewed mind and spirit. Life opened up in ways I could not have imagined not too long ago. With God's unfathomable love diligently working inside my heart and mind, my shackles opened allowing me to journey onward. I attended church once again, something I prayed and asked God to make happen. I longed to be in the presence of other followers. It was great to be back in the house of the Lord regardless of my continuous setbacks. God knew I was seeking His word and ways and He was the only one who truly knew my heart and intense struggles.

"But those who hope in the Lord will renew their strength. They will sour on wings like eagles, they will run and not grow weary, they will walk and not be faint." —Isaiah 40:31 (NIV)

My revival arrived in time for me to attend a special event: Stephine's high school graduation. How sweet it was when the day had finally arrived. I never thought I would still be alive to participate. I always prayed and asked God to keep me alive long enough to see her graduate, and sure enough He came through big time. No words could ever describe the awesome experience of being alive and alert to witness this cornerstone-taking place in Stephine's life. My mind and heart were in a state of pure bliss. No medicine in the world could have granted this awesome sentiment. I knew it was God! You may think this is just a normal occurrence during one's life but, for me, it was an exceptional gift from God.

As if graduation was not enough, I enjoyed a fine meal as well. A group of us attending the graduation made dinner reservations afterward. There were fourteen of us: Stephine, Rob, Stephine's boy friend, and several members of his family. I never thought I would be well enough to attend something like that. In fact, I was so refreshed on the inside that I naturally felt comfortable with my outer shell. That night, there was no phobia or "ugly mirror images" to deal with. I also enjoyed ordering a scrumptious meal from the menu without worrying about the calories and if I would have time to walk it off afterwards. To be able to relax, smile, and laugh in the company of others was the icing on the cake. To me, the entire day was a testament that God was working miracles in my life.

Upon Stephine's graduation, Rob decided to sell their condominium. When we divorced, he always told me he wanted to stay there until Stephine graduated. He wanted her to remain in the same school district to keep her life as stable as possible. He asked if I would be willing to help them look for a new house, due to my previous real estate experience. I was more than willing to give them a hand at finding the perfect house. We began to look at houses together. Rob, Stephine, and I went from one place to the next looking for the perfect place. During this process, Rob ended up with a buyer and it made their house search even more urgent. He and Stephine needed to vacate the condominium by the end of September. House after house after house, none felt right.

Then one day Rob called and asked if I would go with him, once again, to look at another house. Of course, I said yes, because I was anxious for them to find a place they liked. As soon as I stepped into the house, I knew that this was the one. The house had an amazing tranquil feel. When I looked out the sliders leading onto the huge wooden deck, overlooking the beautiful landscaped yard, I imagined Stephine enjoying bonfires with her friends. I knew Rob really liked the house by the smile on his face. There was no doubt he was to purchase it. He placed an offer the same day. The sellers accepted Rob's offer and the packing and moving began.

I was happy for them and knew this stage of their lives would be a new beginning of growth and change. Stephine preparing to attend her first year of college, Rob receiving a higher position at work, and both having a new place to call home was marvelous. They were both excited about the next phase of their lives. Everything fell into place perfectly for them and I was grateful to be a part of it.

However, I sensed it was time for me to make life changes as well.

Lord, No words can express my utmost gratitude to You. Although I had been plagued with many troubles, as I sought refuge under Your wings, You miraculously delivered me, little by little, from my so-called foes. Thank You, Lord, for revealing truth to me in the areas in which I was blinded, in denial, or just didn't realize to be an out-of-control area in my life. Holy Spirit, I thank You for Your continuous help in this surrendering process. Amen

- Do you base your self-worth on outward things or the opinion of others? On the other hand, do you base your worth on what God says about you?
- Has God set you free from something recently?
- Has He been opening new doors for you to travel through as you depart from your old ways of living?

Nineteen

Death Comes Knocking Again

Having to make life-altering decisions while still emotionally unstable, tossed me into utter confusion. *Should I remain in Connecticut and end my relationship with Dave or is it time for me to move back to Florida and settle down with him? Who will help Christina get back and forth from college? Who will help Rob and Stephine with the new home?* I feared making the wrong choice, not trusting my mind or emotions. They failed me before and I did not want to be misguided again. I did not want to sadden those I cherished most: Christina, Stephine, Rob, or Dave. During the three years back in Connecticut, regardless of my limitations with the BDD, I knew I deposited goodness into their lives, making my decision much harder. In addition, the long distance relationship Dave and I remained in was tearing me apart. Exhausted from the separation, I knew it was time to close the gap. Terrible distress blanketed me during the weeks I sought to make a clear-cut decision. *Should I stay or should I go?*

Along with my deepening relationship with beloved ones, another love was intensifying. I knew my spiritual journey with God was growing because the sermons I tuned into via television and radio were no longer filling me as they once did. Something deep within my heart prompted me to step out of the shell I barricaded myself in and stretch for more. I felt a deeper correlation with God as I stepped out of my dark hiding place into His light. Attending church, regardless of the struggle in the bathroom, brought me the additional encouragement I longed for: acknowledging I was on the proper path to recovery, healing, and my destiny.

Over the course of time, I learned what a wonderful person Rob was. He devoted his entire life to raising Stephine. He became a dear friend to me. This heartfelt reality grew during the time I helped him with selling the condominium and the search of their new home. I never thought by doing so I would develop such feelings. This confused me even more. I saw a need in Stephine and Rob's lives, possibly the role I once held. Yet I also recognized the wishes in Dave's life too. He was anxiously waiting to enjoy the new house he had purchased for our future. *God, what should I do? Which way do I go? I do not want to hurt any of them.*

When Rob found the new house, I knew it was the right one but I could not understand why I felt as if I belonged there too. For some reason, I believed I was the one to turn this house into a "home" for them. I also thought it was my responsibility to make them aware of God. With these beliefs stuck in my mind and heart, I became confused as I thought about Dave and making our house in Florida a "home" for us. I became double-minded and my heart wept as my heartstrings were pulled in different directions. Conviction stirred my spirit demanding that I stop wrestling with the issue and make a straightforward decision.

"If any of you lacks wisdom, he should ask God, who gives generously to all without finding fault, and it will be given to him. But when he asks, he must believe and not doubt, because he who doubts is like a wave of the sea, blown and tossed by the wind. That man should not think he will receive anything from the Lord; he is a double-minded man, unstable in all he does." —James 1:5-8 (NIV)

Confusion, confusion, and more confusion settled into my head. *What should I do? I am still so deeply ill. I do not want to hurt any of them with my illness.* Still hesitant and uncertain, I forged ahead and mailed a two-month notice to my landlord advising her that I would be vacating on or about October 30th.

I decided to relocate to Florida in spite of my indecisiveness. I convinced myself that moving to Florida to be with Dave was the best thing to do. I decided to suck it up. I buried my emotions and continued to follow through with my plans to move to Florida.

Regardless of my inner turmoil, I still desired to help Rob and Stephine settle into their new home before heading to Florida. Stephine and I unpacked boxes in her bedroom. I was happy, and delighted to be of service. We enjoyed decorating her new room, displaying her trophies, pictures, and snow globe collection. As I placed the objects on the shelves, I reminisced over the fond memories. Days of watching her cheerlead, seeing her face light up while unwrapping each snow globe I gave her, and witnessing her blossom into a beautiful young lady. She did not say anything to me about my move. She was hurt the last time I left and it took her a while to rebuild her trust in me when I returned. Sure enough, three years later, I was repeating the same journey. I knew it was a sensitive subject so I did not say anything either. While we continued to unpack, she asked if I could decorate the other rooms in the house, stating her dad did not really know how to decorate. Filled with sentiment I told her that it wasn't my place to decorate. Her dad needed to decide how he would like to have it look since this was his house. I suggested she be creative and help him with the other rooms. She simply sighed as we carried on, getting her room in order.

Content with all I accomplished that day–unpacking, cleaning, and tidying things up–I headed out the door feeling blessed. The energy throughout my body and the inner peace abiding my mind made me well aware that God was with me. However, as I drove down the street, back to my place, to pack my belongings for the move to Florida, grief and a sense of great loss stirred within. *How can I leave? Dave is flying up in several days to help me move. I love them all, yet I am still too ill to be with any of them. I would rather be dead than put them through the heartache I am feeling.* At this crisis point, I could not face the fact of moving on in any direction. *How can I live with Dave in Florida while feeling guilty for abandoning Stephine, Christina, and Rob? How can I live a joyful life in Connecticut feeling awful over deserting Dave?*

How stupid was I to turn into a liquor store to buy a six-pack of beer? I lied to myself with the excuse that it might make the packing go easier. Why I thought I could handle a few beers was beyond my sanity. My last drink was well over three years ago. It was a remnant of my old nature and not a part of the new person God was creating me to be. However, Satan knew my area of weakness as he tempted me, *"Surely a six pack of beer will help you. It will not harm you. Go ahead and get some."* Acting on dire emotions and falling into temptation, I went ahead and purchased the beer. What a huge blunder.

"Be self-controlled and alert. Your enemy the devil prowls around like a roaring lion looking for someone to devour."
—1 Peter 5:8 (NIV)

As soon as I entered my apartment, I opened a beer and gulped it down within a few minutes. As I pulled out a few empty boxes and wrapped some items, I grabbed another beer. As the alcohol began to numb me, I lost control of my last grasp of sanity as toxic emotions erupted. I desired to be dead. *I do not want to hurt any of my loved ones. The BDD is still a huge problem. I do not know what to do.* More sorrow blanketed my mind and heart as the alcohol pushed me into further despair.

I stopped packing and drank a few more beers. My suicide mission began. I grabbed hold of the book I had been working on–this book–and wrote a goodbye letter to Bishop J, at the church I attended. I do not know why I wrote this final goodbye letter to him, but I asked him to please have my almost completed book published, knowing it might help others out of darkness. After writing the letter to him, I wrote a letter to both Dave and Rob. I apologized to them for all I had put them through with my highs and lows and for not being able to be all I had hoped to be for them. What a mess! What a mess! What a mess my hurting soul grew into. Shame, guilt, and feeling so inadequate to meet the needs of others overpowered me. I hated breaking anyone else's heart, not giving any thought to my own.

With my final goodbye letters in order, I phoned my mother. In extreme dismay, I told her I just could not take it anymore. I expressed that I could not stomach deciding on whether to stay or move. The indecisiveness to end my relationship with Dave or the guilt, shame, and remorseful feelings of leaving my daughters again was killing me. Crying hysterically, I yelled that the pain was terrible and I was ending my life. All these highly intoxicated emotions led me to death's door yet again.

When I hung up the phone with Mom, I swallowed all the prescription medications I had, followed by a mega size bottle of aspirin. I grabbed the goodbye letters, my unpublished book, and rushed out to my car hoping to make it to the church parking lot before death took over. I planned to park my car in the lot while I remained in it. I anticipated someone finding my lifeless corpse, resting in peace, the following day. As soon as I entered the parking lot everything became fuzzy, a blur. I knew I had to park quickly before I blacked out. I did not want to be found until it was final. When I parked, I made certain my manuscript and the farewell letters were easily visible. I laid them on the front seat next to me. Stillness settled in as dimness took over.

Something within my inner core led me to reach out in despair and leave my last desires and good intentions in the hands of Bishop J. Surely he was the only person I trusted with these items. I respected him to the fullest and I hoped and prayed he would honor my last wishes. I intended to never awake again, yet I did not want my untold story to be lost. I knew God placed it in my heart to write this book and once published it could help other hurting souls. I just did not know how I could accomplish this dream with Satan on my shoulder nearly every step of the way.

Had I known driving into that parking lot would actually save my life, I would not have done it. I was on a straightforward mission to end it. I was conscious long enough to park my car safely in the lot before unconsciousness took over. *God, forgive me. Please take me home. I seek to enter your Heavenly gates.* Everything else that occurred is a blank—until my eyes opened and I found myself laying in yet another hospital bed. *Damn it! I am still alive.* No casket enclosed me. Blurred strangers in green, blue, and white hospital scrubs circled me, chanting, "Barbara wake up, Barbara wake up." As my consciousness returned, the only ones I recognized in the room were Christina, and Bishop J. The hospital staff continued to administer aid while Christina and Bishop J. informed me that everything was going to be okay. I don't recall much more as I drifted in and out of consciousness.

I have no idea what happened during the first few hours in the hospital. However, when I regained consciousness, my arms and legs were strapped to the bedrails because of my severe combativeness. Needles protruded from my arms, monitors hummed all around me, and Christina sat by my bedside. She remained calm through the ordeal, yet I felt powerless, ashamed, and embarrassed, unsuccessful yet again. Her soft words and moist eyes demonstrated she was relieved that I hadn't died. This suicide attempt shocked her more than the others because of its level of severity. I discovered later that I had almost succeeded this time.

With no recollection of what transpired, Christina filled in the gaps. She stated, "Mom you walked into the church and entered a women's Bible study taking place."

"I didn't go into the church. I stayed in my car and everything went black," I defiantly told her.

"Mom it didn't end there. You got out of your car and went into the church. Then the women in the Bible study phoned Bishop J and 911 because of your condition."

"I still don't believe you. I know I blacked out in my car."

"Mom, how do you think you got here if you didn't get out of the car and go into the church? I am telling you the paramedics were called and they brought you here. You can believe what you want but that's what happened. You went into the church."

"I don't know how I got here. I'm not sure what happened after I passed out." To this day, I still have no recollection of entering the church or being transported to the hospital. *Had there not been a women's Bible study taking place, would I still be alive?* What led me to go there? Why? Why? Why? I ask myself at this very moment. The one thing that strikes my heart is the word "connection." I always felt like a foreigner, I did not fit in anywhere or belong to anyone. Yet there was something there! I felt that special, unique belonging within this church. In my heart, I knew this congregation of believers trusted in the same God I believed in. I felt a God–given union yet I often battled in despair trying to make it through the front doors because of the dreadful BDD. Maybe this is one of the reasons I decided to end my life as close to the church as possible.

The first few days in ICU were torturous as the nurses pumped the necessary fluids into my deprived body in order for it to function again. The IV potassium drip burned like acid as it flowed into my vein. Even though they diluted the serum, it remained extremely painful. An intern wanted to administer the potassium at a higher strength to speed my recovery. I knew this would cause me greater agony. I overheard one of the nurses stating she was not going to administer the higher strength dosage of potassium because she did not want to put me in greater pain. She suggested waiting to see if the level would rise. She came in to check the IV and suggested I not drink anything so the potassium would not be flushed from my system. Over the course of several more excruciating hours, my potassium level rose to an acceptable level. They also noted I was fortunate that my kidneys improved, not needing dialysis.

Dave immediately flew to Connecticut when Christina informed him of what had transpired. I was glad to see him when he entered the hospital room, knowing he would help me through this terrible ordeal. No one else from my family visited, except for Christina. I talked with Rob for a few minutes over the phone and he wished me well. Dave was very concerned for my welfare, anxious to move me to Florida to recuperate. However, my fate remained in the hands of the doctors who were in no rush to release me.

I remained in the ICU while my pain ridden, debilitated body recovered. They held me for four long, agonizing days. As my body recuperated, they refused to release me into Dave's care. They were contemplating transporting me directly to a psychiatric facility for further evaluation. They did not want to be liable for another attempt. No matter how much I pleaded with them to release me, they continued to deny my request due to my history of suicide and the severity of this one. Fear encircled me every minute I remained in the hospital. My nerves were shaken by the physical and mental challenges encompassing me.

Sure enough, my worst nightmare arrived when they dropped the bomb. They told me I would be going to another facility for further evaluation and were uncertain for how long. I virtually collapsed when I heard the news. I freaked out envisioning being locked up in a facility against my own will and needing to face my BDD. *I don't want to go. I'm afraid! I'm never going to survive the BDD there.* Filled with insurmountable fear I continued to pray to God for help. My atrocious situation could not get any worse, yet I clung to my faith trusting that God was with me no matter where they sent me.

"God, you're my last chance of the day, I spend the night on my knees before you." —Psalm 88:1 (TM)

Father God, Be merciful to me, O Lord, for I did not know what I was doing. Forgive me for seeking to take my life and for allowing the enemy to ambush me once again. Had I waited patiently to clearly hear from You, I would not have fallen into utter confusion. Though the shadow of death blanketed me, Your unfailing love rescued me. Surely, You must have a mission for me to accomplish and perhaps that is why the enemy has been trying to take me out. May the good works You started within me be carried on to completion for Your glory and kingdom purposes. In Jesus' name I pray, Amen

- Are you stable in your emotions, life, and relationship with God so you can make good, healthy, proper, and wise decisions?
- Do you often sense that you are in a "spiritual battle" because you are persevering in the things God has called you to accomplish?
- Are you aware of your weak spots, areas of sin that can easily cause you to spiral downwards should you dabble in them?

Twenty

Let Me Out of Here

The social worker returned to my room and informed me the ambulance was on its way. As I waited for it to arrive, an inner calmness surrounded me, soothing my traumatized nerves. I shifted from a crippling fear of doom to an unruffled sense of assurance that everything was going to be fine. *God I know this peace is from you. Thank you for calming me down. This situation remains dreadful, but I know I'll make it through with You by my side.*

"Even though I walk through the valley of the shadow of death, I will fear no evil, for you are with me; your rod and your staff they comfort me."— Psalm 23:4 (NIV)

I remained quiet as they wheeled me into the ambulance. The ride took almost a half hour and Dave followed close behind. The paramedic accompanying me could not understand why they were transferring me to this unpleasant psychiatric facility. "Barbara you don't look like the type of person that needs to go to this kind of place. You cannot begin to imagine the kind of people we bring there. Hopefully they won't keep you long."

"I told them I didn't want to go. They said I had no choice. I'm praying I'll get out in a day."

We pulled up in front of the building and the ambulance attendees wheeled me in on a gurney. Right away, the place gave me the creeps. The lobby alone frightened me—security guards, and surveillance cameras posted all over the place. *Is this where they keep Hannibal Lector?* The smell, filth, and thick, discolored Plexiglas separating the visitors entering from the hospital staff made me ill. *It stinks in here. Look at all the trash on the floor. How could they possibly see through that filthy, scratched up window?* As soon as the ambulance attendees brought me into the lobby, authorities from the facility took over.

They tightly strapped me onto one of their gurneys, preventing me from escaping and incurring any injuries during the long ride to the other end of the facility. We journeyed from one extensive corridor to the next–an endless maze as we went up, down, and around the cold dreary hallways. *God, where are they bringing me? This is like a house of horrors.* Staff punched codes into the security devices granting entrance through every solid steel door we approached. Each endless corridor we journeyed through grew colder and darker. It was strange that nobody was in sight. Jokingly I asked if they were bringing me to the basement. Upon arriving at our discreet destination, I heard rattling of keys unlocking the final steel door I would enter. *Oh! No! Are they unlocking the chamber door to a reformatory?*

Thank goodness, I remained peaceful and calm. The unperturbed demeanor I needed to state my case with the intake worker. Dave stayed by my side and helped with the paperwork. Having him present and involved would make a huge difference in my release. With the paperwork completed the hospital staff sorted through my belongings. I felt violated as they inspected each item, dictating what I could keep, what Dave had to take home, and what items they would lock away. The process was degrading, but necessary for the overall safety of the patients, staff, and visitors.

Past visiting hours, Dave was required to leave. I waved goodbye as he exited the solid steel doors. The nurse immediately locked the doors behind him. As I walked to my room, horror spilled from the other rooms—moans, groans, and hostile words transcended from the patient's rooms. *This place gives me the creeps. Who will be in my room?* I was frightened as I continued my journey, carrying the worn-out green and white hospital gowns given to me. The nurse handed me two, advising to put one on frontward and the other backwards. The gowns had neither snaps nor ties remaining and they did not permit patients roaming the hallways exposed. When I arrived at my room, I was pleasantly surprised to find a peaceful old woman as my roommate. *God, thank you!* She kindly introduced herself when I entered. I knew we would be good companions. Within minutes, the facility turned down all the lights, announcing it was time for everyone to go to bed. We quietly settled in.

As I lay awake, I desired to escape through the window. However, I glanced over, and realized steel bars girded the windows. *There is no escaping from this place. God, how will I make it through the BDD tomorrow when I take a shower? The showers down the hallway are disgusting.* I settled down and prayed to God to protect me from this house of horror.

To my surprise, when I awoke the following morning, I heard water running from the bathroom in my room. My roommate was already up preparing for the day. When she came out, she dripped from head to toe. She had just finished taking a shower. She informed me that she was done and I could go in to take a shower. A huge smile lit my face as I headed for the shower in my own room. I thought I would be grooming in the common bathrooms with the other patients. Right away, I knew God was watching out for me; I was placed in one of the only rooms that had a private shower. This blessing made my grooming much smoother than I had hoped or ever imagined. As I finished in the bathroom, I had faith that the rest of the day was going to be fine. Little blessings such as these, a pleasant roommate and a private shower, made me aware that God remained with me even in a dungeon like this. He continued to comfort my inner turmoil as uncertain circumstances unfolded.

With the serenity I now possessed, I recognized the desolation that lingered behind the solid, brick walls of this psychiatric ward. The obscurity that filled this institution was not healthy. I was amazed that a place like this even existed. My heart opened up to the patients roaming the hallways in their filthy hospital gowns, lining up at the nurse's station to take their morning medications. I knew in my heart that the healing most of them needed could not be found in the pills being administered. I was the only one sound enough to speak up and refuse the medication they wanted me to take. To my surprise, the nurses honored my refusal. I believe my good mannerism, high spirits, and alertness made them realize I was not a threat to them or the other patients.

Strict rules required all patients to wear regular clothes upon entering the dining area. No Johnny coats allowed. Sad to say, most of them would have been better off keeping their hospital gowns on. I did not know how long most of them were there for but it looked as though their clothes came out of a dumpster, torn and frayed, huge stains and even human feces covered them. Many patients' fought over each other's food, not liking their own. They snatched items from trays and even out of other patients' hands. I kept a distance searching for a table with quiet patients. Most of them were zoned out, highly medicated, shuffling around the dining area. The housekeeper tried to do her job. Each time she cleaned up a mess, within minutes, several more occurred. She must have known I did not belong there, maybe as I held myself differently. She came over and politely asked my name. She whispered in my ear that she would be praying that God would get me out soon. She recognized His Spirit within me as I professed my high hopes of early release.

Waiting to see the doctor assigned to my case, I became irritated. I did not understand why there was such a delay. Finally, a social worker visited me and explained that my doctor would not be around until tomorrow. I asked why all the other patients were scheduled to be seen and I had to wait. She stated my doctor did not make rounds until a certain day of the week and the other doctors' schedules were completely full. I told her I was not pleased because I was hoping to get out that day.

When visiting hours arrived, I was thrilled to see Dave, the only sound person around to talk with. I explained how awful the place was and I could not wait to be released. I fretted about how long I would be trapped here, yet Dave assured me he would remain by my side regardless. He too agreed how dreary this institution was. Troubled souls pacing the foul-smelling hallways, abandoned and alone, and a staff worn out, depleted by callous working conditions and patients disturbed by life. Many of the patients had no visitors. I counted my blessings and realized how disheartening mental illness can be for many—patients, staff, family, and friends. In spite of the appalling conditions, Dave and I savored the short visiting hours. I rested in the comfort of his arms breathing in the aroma of his cologne.

Excited about the following day when I would plead my case with the doctor assigned to my care, I had a hard time falling asleep. Throughout the night, I prayed to God to release me soon. As the sun rose, so did my spirit. I wanted to be sound-minded meeting the doctor and a light to the hurting patients as long as I was trapped here. When the nurse arrived to bring me down to see the doctor, I did not know what to expect. *Will he let me out of here? Is he going to keep me locked up for several more days, weeks or even months? God, I pray this meeting goes well. I have faith that You will set me free.*

At first, I sensed the meeting was not going well. He did not look me in the face as he asked questions about what took place. While skimming my chart he stated that according to the paperwork in my folder I intended to kill myself. Duh! I could have told him that. As he continued to look over my file, reading my farewell note, he stated he had never encountered such a serious, planned out act of suicide. While interrogating me, he remained eyes down, my file continuing to amuse him. Minutes passed, he finally asked what I was suffering from. I told him a disorder called BDD. Suddenly his attention abruptly shifted into attentiveness and compassion. He placed my folder down, turned his chair towards me, and asked how long I had been dealing with it. "Well over fifteen years and this is the fifth time I tried to kill myself because of it," I responded.

Listening carefully, he became teary eyed, and he apologized for my suffering. He mentioned he was treating a male patient for the same disorder and recently lost him due to suicide. He noted that the case was tough. We chatted for a while and I advised him that the facility was deplorable and I wanted to be released. He agreed, wished me well, and wrote my release orders for the following day. Upon leaving the meeting, I thanked God for aligning me with a doctor who had knowledge of BDD.

"For I am convinced that neither death nor life, neither angels nor demons, neither the present nor the future, nor any powers, neither height nor depth, nor anything else in all creation, will be able to separate us from the love of God that is in Christ Jesus our Lord."
—Romans 8:38-39 (NIV)

The following day, with my belongings packed and release papers awaiting my signature, I realized many of the patients were sad over my quick release because they liked me. Yet, they were glad my steadfast hope of early discharge came as swiftly as I had prayed. My heart understood the pain they faced, yet I knew their care was beyond my ability and only God could minister to their broken spirits and was the true antidote to their healing.

When I spotted Dave waiting for me at the nurse's station, I heaved a huge sigh of relief. He was anxious to return me to my apartment to recuperate and he could pack the rest of my stuff. During the ride, I did not know what was in store for me. The pain that filled my body and mind in the ICU quickly resurfaced, as did the thoughts of moving on. *I'm stuck having to move to Florida. I'm going to have to face saying goodbye to Christina and Stephine. I'm too broken to think clearly at this time.* My nerves unraveled, fraying again at having to move on in life.

The first few days at my apartment were difficult–dreadful, to say the least. My body ached with pain, overwhelm with excruciating soreness due to the horrendous shock it experienced. Just getting up to go to the bathroom hurt. The disbelief that I did not die troubled me too. All the things I did not want to face remained. I choked on the tugging in my heart, the little voice within suggesting I stay in Connecticut. I pushed everything down, way down, so I could pick up the pieces of my broken life and move on.

Father God, In my greatest time of need Your Spirit comforted me. Even in the midst of my own troubles, Your Spirit shined through me as a beacon of Light for others sitting in darkness. Surely, You were working behind the scene, lining me up with a doctor who fully understood the psychological disorder playing havoc in my life. Thank You for setting me free from what could have been a lengthy stay. Neither steal doors nor chains could separate or prevent Your love reaching down to me. I Thank You, Lord. Amen

---

- Have you ever walked through a "valley of darkness" yet felt God's presence within you?
- Do you know that God loves you no matter where you might be in life today?
- He is just one prayer away in helping you break free from whatever holds you captive.

Twenty-One

A Rainbow at the End of the Storm

My heart ached when the time arrived to say goodbye to Christina and Stephine. I suppressed my grief, sorrow, and shame. As their mom, I sought to stand strong and positive. I refused to breakdown in their presence. Christina preferred I relocate to Florida suggesting, "Mom, I think you should give it a chance. After a few months, if you do not like it then move back. Dave will understand."

"I suppose you're right. I will go ahead and give it another try. I will fly up to visit you in a few months. I will call you when I arrive in Florida. I love you."

Stephine on the other hand, guarded herself. She could not comprehend my irrational way of thinking without knowledge of the severity of my BDD and past. I shielded her from it. "Mom, why would you want to kill yourself? You are being selfish trying to take your life. Don't you know I need you?"

"I'm sorry. I did not mean to hurt you. I hope you will keep in touch with me."

"Whatever!" she muttered. With arms folded and a grimace on her face.

I abstained from giving her a hug. My self-destructive behavior offended her and I did not blame her for acting cold and distant. I felt like a wet dog with his tail tucked between his legs as I left her presence. This dumped additional guilt and distress on my already debilitated soul.

I struggled to remain strong on the outside as Dave and I traveled to Florida. I sought to protect him from the desolation looming within me. In an effort to hide my tears from Dave, I closed my eyes pretending to be asleep. However, they trickled out regardless. Nearly every hour I wrote in my prayer journal expressing my utmost concerns to God. Prayer after prayer I asked Him to wipe away my sadness and to comfort my daughters as well. With each passing mile, my body ached more and more. I did not now how to process the dreadful feelings twirling inside of me. The humongous load of grief, sorrow, and loss suppressing me outweighed the full load of cargo we hauled. Dave remained sympathetic through the trip as though I was a fragile egg ready to break.

The move backfired. For seven months, I grew weary from my broken heart, the out of control BDD disorder, and the unavoidable "knowing" I harbored in sin cohabitating with Dave. Depleted mentally, physically, and spiritually I sank into another endless abyss. I traveled from one doctor to the next, searching for answers and relief from the pain terrorizing my entire body. Finding and receiving relief for all I suffered was inaccessible. As I continued to search for an antidote, I aroused to the possibility that perhaps the pain and discomfort was not physical. According to the vast material I read, the main source, my Bible, maybe the culprit was mental anguish and spiritual discord.

I despised living in Florida and rejected the lovely house Dave bought for our future. Nearly every day I poured my grief and sorrow on him. This poor management of my toxic emotions led me into further despair, for I knew Dave did not deserve this mistreatment. He meant no harm. I buried myself in the guilt, shame, and condemnation mounted up inside, which increased my BDD. The hideous image in my mirror only dispersed tyranny. *Mirror, mirror on the wall, who is the ugliest of them all? It is you, Barbara, who is the ugliest of them all. Disgrace follows you wherever you roam. You will never escape from this prison.*

Out of dire desperation, I turned to the Internet for help. I stumbled across a website that hosted a great deal of information pertaining to BDD. The site offered insight but more importantly, I found a support group. My heart sympathized with the members. Their pain and sorrow felt so familiar; I suffered it too. Responding to the forum with positive support paid off. Each time I reached out to the group a huge wave of encouragement dispensed bringing relief to my despondent soul. Although most of them talked about doctors, medications, and various treatments, I trusted in God for my healing. Many of the visitors were actually family members looking for help for their loved ones suffering from this terrible disorder. They longed for a better life for their beloved one. They feared losing their son or daughter by way of suicide. *Someone has to bring this disorder to the forefront. Too many lives are hiding behind closed doors suffering from this "ugly" mirror syndrome.*

During this wretched season of life, I continued to pour my ambitions into this book. Besides working on the book, I kept in contact with my daughters via phone, email, and snail mail too, doing my best to nurture and encourage them through their own challenges and heartaches. I also developed a newfound friendship with a lovely, older woman named Fran. We met on a Christian women's devotional website. She became my spiritual mother even though only via the Internet. We both knew in our hearts that our friendship was God ordained. She poured so much of God's love into my wretched soul as I shared my afflictions with her. She never ceased praying for me. I believe God deliberately deposited Fran into my life to aid me through this desolate period.

Numerous times, I failed making it to church on Sunday mornings. Hour after hour shackled to the hideous image in my mirror and the lies filling my mind nearly destroyed me. I knew healing awaited me, yet the BDD continued to pull me down. Many times, I mustered up the energy and drove to church regardless. However, crippling fear, ugliness, and dismay prevented me from going in. Parked outside the church, I sat in my car reading my Bible as I cried out to God. I did not let Dave in on what I was doing; I wanted him to think I made it to church fine and that I did not let the atrocious attacks get the best of me. However, one Sunday the attack was very bad. Dave did not know what to do and suggested we go to the beach for a morning walk. I agreed in spite of how disgusting I thought I looked. To our surprise as we walked the beach an adorable little church floated by. Immediately my heart fluttered as I looked up to say thank you to God. Both Dave and I were filled with joy as I professed with a huge smile on my face, "I couldn't make it to church so God arranged to have one float by." Soon after, we realized the floating church was used for weddings taking place on the water. As we drove home, I recognized that God was still with me even though I might have drifted off course.

In spite of my good intentions, seeking to make it to church, working on my book and reaching out to the BDD sufferers, my health continued to deteriorate. I longed for healing and rest, yet found no reprieve for my weary soul. Then one horrible day, I encountered the worst, the ugliest, and the wickedest BDD attack ever. I went berserk! The bottled up emotions piling up inside of me exploded. The insurmountable pain, guilt, and condemnation stacking up erupted like a ferocious volcano. The gruesome vision appearing in my mirror fed my mind one atrocious lie after another. *You are a rotten mother. You abandoned your daughters. You are a disgrace. A hypocrite living in sin. You are the most sinister human alive.* The Tasmanian devil broke loose.

Sad to say, Dave received the brunt of my ferocious whirlwind of toxic emotions. He became the central target as these ugly feelings fled from me. Seven months of agony, self-hatred, and misery boiled over into an explosive expression of rage and anger. The dark abyss I trudged and the unbearable BDD attack propelled me into a death defying "fight or flight" mode in order to escape the horrible "inner prison" I remained locked in.

Out of control and flabbergasted beyond measure, the pictures on the wall shook when I slammed the door shut to our study. I grabbed the nearest pen and pad and wrote a letter to Dave. I noted I needed to get back to Connecticut as soon as possible. I explained I missed my girls beyond measure. Secondly, I emphasized I could not endure living in sin. I needed my own place. I also made note that I did not expect his help with getting back as he suffered this route once before. This overwhelming episode was the pivotal point, which forced me into action. *I cannot go on living like this. I have to get back home.*

I trembled as I handed the letter to Dave. I feared his response. I left the room, giving him time to read and digest the news. After he read it, we sat down and discussed an unarguable outcome. He accepted that I needed to get back, and I could not guarantee I would ever return. Twice I tried it and both times, it failed. We concluded I would return to Connecticut.

Depleted from the ordeal, I crawled into bed crying out to God. I prayed for Him to bring me back to where He desired. Concerned about money, furniture, and unable to hold a job due to the BDD disorder overwhelmed me as I cried myself to sleep. *Where am I going to live? How will I support myself? My health is deteriorating and this BDD is unfathomable.* Dave kept silent the rest of the night, giving me space to quiet down and pray.

The following morning I roused with the utter peace only God bequeaths. The awe-inspiring energy, calm demeanor, and lack of crippling body aches could not have manifested from anywhere else. The peace bestowed upon me was the "something" I lacked since I relocated to Florida. A miracle transpired as I slept—the renewal of my mind and restoration of my body. In a twinkling of an eye, restitution came, granting me the strength, ability, and determination to move forward in heading home by the end of the week. *I have faith that all will work out fine. I need not worry. God will provide.*

Everything swiftly fell into place as I planned to move back. I contacted my previous landlord to find out if she had an available apartment. Sure enough, she just so happened to receive a letter from a tenant desiring to terminate her lease due to financial problems. It worked out perfect for all of us. She sent the lease and keys via FedEx overnight and I ended up leasing the apartment a few days later. Right away, I acknowledged God stood behind the scene helping. I thanked Him for providing me with an apartment. He delivered me right back into the same apartment building I moved out of several months prior, close to my daughters and church too.

In spite of misdirecting my fury at Dave, he still desired to help with the move. I apologized for all I put him through; I did not mean to harm him. Through this ordeal, I learned what true love meant. Dave stood by my side through this dark arena and the many other unpleasant upheavals too. I recognized his true devotion to me, married or not. We pulled together as a team, packing the vehicle heading north. Dave ached by my leaving, yet remained hopeful that our relationship would survive as I fulfilled the longings in my heart.

"Love is patient, love is kind. It does not envy, it does not boast, it is not proud. It is not rude, it is not self-seeking, it is not easily angered, it keeps no record of wrongs. Love does not delight in evil but rejoices in truth. It always protects, always trusts, always hopes, always perseveres." —1 Corinthians 13: 4-7 (NIV)

When I entered the new apartment, I knew God redirected me right back to where He desired. Yet I sulked over the possibility of never seeing Dave again. Right away, I knew I needed to remain focused on the present and not seek to plan the future. Dave helped unpack my belongings and made certain I settled into the apartment nicely. He stayed for a few days and helped paint, clean, and shop before boarding his flight. I graciously and humbly accepted his steadfast support.

Upon arriving at the airport, Dave kissed me goodbye and whispered, "I believe this is not the end. I hope everything works out for you. I'll give you a call when I return home."

I responded, "Thanks for all your help. I have to take things one day at a time. I hope you have a safe trip back. I'll talk to you later."

Driving home from the airport, a tidal wave of emotions slammed me. For some reason I lost my assurance that, I had made the right choice. Moving back to Connecticut, pulling away from Dave, and many other uncertainties bombarded my mind. Thoughts of fleeing back to Florida, thinking I would never overcome the BDD so I could work, and visions of hanging myself coiled and twisted in my mind. I was afraid of the unknown and fearful of moving on due to my limitations. Thus, I clung to my faith in God to help me through this changeover.

Having privacy did not lift the BDD disorder. It remained a crippling defect, a "thorn in my flesh." *God, will I ever be free from this horrible disorder?* For two tear-filled weeks, I cried out to God for help and protection. I continuously reached out to my friend, Fran, asking her for prayer. She knew the spiritual battle taking place in my life. Every night I thanked God for getting me through the day alive. Every single time I stepped out in faith to move upwards, it seemed like disorder erupted. Through Bible reading, prayer, and Fran's keen spiritual insight and wisdom, I determined to keep pressing on. God brought me this far and I had faith He would deliver me from this ambush too.

Thank goodness, I persevered with two very important issues: returning to church and seeking employment, both imperative for my survival. I sought to accomplish these goals regardless of the BDD and fear of going out in public. I stomped through and blessed rewards followed. Determined to attend church despite the affliction in the bathroom, another BDD snare, a pleasant surprise awaited me. A blessing I never expected.

During service, Bishop J mentioned a water baptism ceremony-taking place outside the cathedral that afternoon. He stated, "Whoever would like to participate in the baptismal ceremony may still join in regardless if you had not signed up."

My heart pounded like a drum when I heard the announcement, yearning to participate. Ever since I accepted Christ, I desired to partake in water baptism. I never followed through with my good intention out of narcissism, the stupid BDD, and how awful I would look coming out of the water.

Pride, another deadly sin, coerced me to respond this way. However, this blessed Sunday, I responded to the invitation without worrying about my looks. I humbly committed myself to partake in this sacred opportunity. I refused to allow my old mindset to keep me from doing that which I whole-heartedly desired to accomplish.

Thrilled, I rushed to my apartment, swapped clothes, and grabbed a towel. Driving back to church, I prayed. *God, Thank you for providing me with this opportunity to partake in this blessed ceremony.* As soon as I returned, I sought my spot in line. Standing in admiration to my beloved Lord, I imagined God glancing down at me with the biggest smile on His face. I was about to achieve an aspiration I had always yearned to fulfill. Within minutes, I would carry out my ambition.

I merged into the serene setting surrounding us, anxiously waiting to hear my name announced. A white trellised gazebo crowned the three-tier cascading baptismal pools. An arched bridge divided the first two upper tiers, a water fountain sprung from the middle, and stone white steps led into the bottom tier where submergence takes place. *I cannot wait to get down there.* A sweet harmony filled the air—birds chirping and water flowing from each tier. Huge green trees bordered the breathtaking landscape, pink, purple, and red blooming bushes bejeweled the grounds. Pure white statues, railings, and stone outlined the edges of the warm brick pathway we journeyed. A large audience witnessed the ceremony taking place.

Finally, my turn arrived! I heard my name announced and climbed down the ladder leading into the baptismal pool. Emerged in the water, I began to float like a cloud in the sky. Two pastors clothed in white robes stood in the water; they grasped hold of my hands gently pulling me towards them. As these servants of God held me, I felt like a little angel. *Am I in heaven?* Leaning backwards into the water, peace, joy, and accord filled me. I sensed a deep cleansing. Like a strand of hair, if not cleansed from daily dirt and grim it becomes dull, flat, and lifeless in appearance. Once washed, cleansed, and clarified it becomes clean, shiny, and vibrant. Arising from the water, gazing into the sky as the snow-white clouds parted, warm rays of grace and mercy from the blazing July sun touched my face. I imagined the angels above singing, Halleluiah! Halleluiah! Hall-ee-luu-iahh! Exiting the water, I joined up with the other soaked partakers watching the remaining water baptisms, not once giving any thought to my drenched look. It did not matter. What mattered more—I accomplished a God ordained aspiration, in spite of my BDD.

"Repent and be baptized, everyone of you, in the name of Jesus Christ for the forgiveness of your sins. And you will receive the gift of the Holy Spirit. The promise is for you and your children and for all who are far off—for all whom the Lord our God will call."
—Acts 2:38-39 (NIV)

Overly delighted I quickly returned home excited to share the good news. As soon as I entered, I booted up my computer and rushed an email to Fran. She knew how badly I desired to make it to church, fully aware of my struggle with the BDD. I knew she would jump for joy when she read the email, informing her I made it to church and to my surprise was baptized too. Her endless prayers and my determination produced a divine "miracle." I shared my joy with Dave as well. He was glad to hear that I made it to church. He knew how many times I failed and the heartache and grief that generally followed. I challenged my two worst foes, the BDD and going out in public, and I won! More importantly, out of obedience to God, I let go of my pride and humbly plunged into the water baptism without obsessing over my appearance upon exiting the water. I left my vanity at home locked up in the bathroom with my adversaries.

A few days later, I received a call regarding a job I applied for a week prior. It was a part-time position in a gym for women only. I went for the interview and they hired me the following day. I accepted the few days offered. However, I worried about my BDD. Yet I knew I needed to persevere in order to make ends meet and to set a good example for my daughters. Aware of my weakness, I chose to confront it.

I knew God opened these doors of opportunities so I stepped out in faith, doing my part. I never imagined I would receive one blessing, after the next. My relationship with Christina and Stephine grew stronger, Rob and I remained friends, and my relationship with Dave survived.

Dear God, Thank you for this new beginning, I hope I do not mess up again. Thank You that Your Word is true and that all things do work together for good to those who love You. Lord, Jesus Christ, I thank You for making a way for the forgiveness of my sins, for spiritual cleansing, and making me clean again. God, I thank You for the gift of Your Holy Spirit who resides within me. May such promise be given to my beloved children and to all who are afar off—for You do not desire for anyone to perish. In Jesus' name I pray, Amen

---

- If you are a Believer in the Lord, have you publicly demonstrated your faith in Him by partaking in water baptism? If not, why?
- How has your "love walk" been lately?
- Do you have an anger problem that needs addressing?

"Open for me the gates of righteousness; I will enter and give thanks to the Lord."

—Psalm 118:19 (NIV)

Twenty-Two

Keep Pressing On

Embracing the new opportunities God opened—relationships, church, and work—brought blessed rewards and daunting challenges too. Joy filled my heart in all three areas at first, however, as time evolved the BDD created opposition again. I wondered if unknown sin, my archenemy, Satan, or maybe God's disciplining hand brought on the turbulence. The upheaval was unpleasant, yet I chose to press on no matter how crippled, lame, or defeated I felt. I longed to live a righteous, well-balanced life and desired to share God's love with others. *God, reveal to me what is wrong. What is causing this ugly mayhem again?*

While working the part-time position at the gym, *Curves for Women*, the BDD erupted as weeks passed. My position as a fitness coach required me to stand in the center of a circular exercise circuit in order to observe, correct, and encourage the women during their thirty-minute workout. As I paced the floor assisting the members, nearly all of them interrogated me. They sought to know me, asking one question after the next. At first, the probing did not bother me, but as days and weeks passed, I grew to dislike the nonstop assessment. Apprehension brewed inside of me, stimulating the manifestation of the BDD.

Shortly after my hire my boss dismissed an employee, the members adored. A handful of the members were furious, downright angry over my boss's decision to let her go. Since I was given her hours, I unfortunately took the brunt of their fury. Having to work with this strife caused me great discomfort and the BDD grew out of control. Once again, I pulled out my props–a phony smile and a hat. The horror in the bathroom was so great I reverted to wearing a baseball cap nearly every day I worked.

At first, the women were fine with it, but as time passed, a few of the callous members dropped remarks. "Barbara, why do you wear that hat all the time? Did you get a bad haircut? Barbara, why don't you take that thing off?" Each trespass propelled me into further misery. Inwardly I struggled with their disturbing comments. Yet I chose to maintain a cheerful outward appearance. I repressed and hid my inner turmoil in order to carry out my job well. My boss was pleased with my work performance and, thank goodness, the majority of the members appreciated my enthusiasm and dedication to their successful workouts.

The despair mounting inside of me provoked me into suicidal thinking again. The atrocious thoughts surfaced every time I worked. A combination of the rising BDD, hiding the affliction, and exposure to social scrutiny intensified the suicidal inclinations. Each evening shift after all the clients left I cleaned the uninhabited facility. The high steel cross bar beckoned me–visions of hanging limp and dead swamped me. In order to escape these daunting thoughts of terror I often shifted my thoughts towards my daughters and Dave. *I have to get home to call Dave. He is going to be worried if he does not hear from me.* Each night as I escaped the ghastly deception, locking the entrance doors behind me, I gazed upon the starlit sky and thanked God for rescuing me.

In spite of the BDD, I persisted in going to church. However, each week the war grew harder, forcing me to hibernate once again, surrendering to watching sermons via television. Discontented with this outcome, I decided to challenge myself after a few weeks of isolation. I longed to be in the house of the Lord. Sad to say, I struggled with the distorted, hideous image in my mirror as I prepared for church. The hours spent in the bathroom were excruciating as I fought to groom myself. Tired, weary, and nearly defeated I succumbed to shoving my baseball cap on and drove to church regardless. I sought to bring my accumulating tithes and knew I desperately needed prayer.

Terrorized by the onslaught in the bathroom and humiliated by the need to use a baseball cap, I remained captive in my car, frozen in fear of rejection. Instead of going in, I listened to a T.D. Jakes *Women Thou Art Loosed* CD. I wept the entire time I stayed in my car, parked in the middle of the church parking lot for over two hours. I believed my healing awaited me through those church doors. Still deeply wounded and disturbed, I drove to my church's bookstore hoping to drop off my tithe and maybe even stumble across a book that might offer some hope.

Upon entering the bookstore, a friendly woman greeted me. "Hello my name is Joann. Is there anything I could help you with?"

"Hi. My name is Barbara. I am just browsing right now. Thank you."

Overwhelmed, I struggled to hold back my tears. However, within minutes, the floodgates opened and tears streamed down my face. I sensed God's presence, His closeness as I searched through the blessed merchandise on display.

My heart quivered as soon as I spotted an inspirational plaque. Tears flowed when I picked it up and read the all too familiar passage.

"And a woman was there who had been subject to bleeding for twelve years, but no one could heal her. She came up behind him and touched the edge of his cloak, and immediately her bleeding stopped."
—Luke 8:43-44 (NIV)

I related my affliction to the woman mentioned above and shown in the plaque. As she sought her healing, I believed that Jesus would heal me too. Wiping the tears from my face, I humbly walked up to the check out counter.

"Did you find what you were looking for? Is there anything else?" Joann asked.

"Do you have a tithing envelope? I couldn't make it into church and I want to give my tithe." I replied, holding back my tears. Caught by surprise and not sure if she heard me correctly, she repeated my unusual request.

"I hope you have a tithing envelope." I responded as the floodgates of my heart opened and tears let go. Realizing how serious the situation was, Joann handed me tissues and immediately searched her purse for a tithing envelope.

"I'm sorry to inconvenience you like this. I have been battling with a horrible disorder that makes me think I am too ugly to go out in public. I had to put this hat on in order to go out today. Nobody could ever imagine the battle I'm in." Holding the plaque in my hand, I declared, "Just like this lady mentioned in the Bible, I'm pressing on for my healing too."

"Barbara, I found an envelope. Here you go."

"Thank you so much. I hope you do not mind taking it over to the church. I'm so embarrassed."

Joann replied, "I'm more than willing to take it over. What you have done here today is unbelievable. I never encountered such a genuine, sincere act of obedience. My heart goes out for you. Please let me pray for you."

Joann and I talked in greater length. By the time we were done, we both knew God arranged our blessed encounter. It was the first Sunday they decided to open the bookstore due to the upcoming holidays. No one else entered, granting us the opportunity to talk almost until closing. The peace and joy flowing through my heart upon leaving the sacred bookstore rekindled the Spirit within me.

"Come to me, all you who are weary and burdened, and I will give you rest. Take my yoke upon you and learn from me, for I am gentle and humble in heart, and you will find rest for your souls. For my yoke is easy and my burden is light." —Mathew 11:28-30 (NIV)

Determined to make it to church the following Sunday, I went shopping for an acceptable looking hat to wear. Just in case. The pink baseball cap I often wore was suitable for work but not church. I searched several stores but was unsuccessful in finding one I liked. I continued my search, and discovered an adorable black felt hat. My face lit up when I tried it on. I knew it was the perfect one.

Sunday arrived and I went to church with my new, little black hat on. Joy and peace surrounded me as I embraced the awesome service. I humbly wore my new hat and a lovely, black, hand knit scarf Fran had made for me. She had prayed over it while she knitted it and she then mailed it to me as a Christmas gift. During service, I glanced among the congregation and noticed others wearing hats too, some similar to the one I wore. Joann at the bookstore was right. Others wore hats to church, especially in the cold, snowy, winter months.

Service ended and I rushed over to the bookstore hoping to see Joann. As soon as I entered, I spotted her. Right away, she knew I had made it to church because of my shimmering glow. We chatted for awhile, relishing in God's faithfulness to those who diligently seek Him. When I returned home, I shared the awesome news with my devoted friend, Fran. She relished in my triumph. I believed her intercessory prayers and my perseverance plowed the way for this victory.

However, suicidal thoughts continued to bombard my mind. I could not imagine treading through life this way anymore. With such evil thoughts invading my mind at work, it was imperative that I escape. I did not want to die! I did not want to hang myself inside my work place, especially now that I was going to be a grandmother. Yes, my oldest daughter, Christina announced she was pregnant and the baby was due in July. Excited about the news, I determined to triumph over all my afflictions and woes, continuing to seek God for aid and guidance.

Dave, worried for my safety and wellness, asked me to spend a few months in Florida after celebrating the holidays with Christina and Stephine. I mentioned that I was contemplating quitting my job at *Curves* due to the atrocious thoughts bombarding my mind there. He thought I would benefit from getting away. I informed my boss that I needed a few months off. I did not tell him I needed the time away in order to escape the toxic emotions twirling through my mind. I simply mentioned that I was going to spend a few months in Florida with my fiancée. My boss was willing to hold my position until I returned. He valued my work ethics and a majority of the members waited my return as well.

Dave flew up for Christmas and we headed to Florida shortly after. We locked up my apartment, knowing I would be heading back to Connecticut after the cold winter months. Yet, I did not believe I would return to my place of employment, where the evil thoughts of suicide haunted me. I hoped time away would aid my recovery.

Lord, I trust that there are good reasons for all that I have endured. Surely, Lord, You would not have rescued me repeatedly without a good purpose. In time, I am confident You will reveal more to me as You see fit. Thank You for opening up windows of opportunity as I diligently persevered in doing my part. God, I am your servant–may Your will be done in and through me. Amen

- Do you believe that the Lord is able to heal you?
- Do you believe in the power of prayer?
- Do you enjoy going to church?

"The Lord is with me; he is my helper. I will look in triumph on my enemies."

—Psalm 118:7 (NIV)

Twenty-three

A Light at the End of the Tunnel

Dave and I enjoyed our trip to Florida. It took me a month to recover from the stress at work. The time away served me well. My suicidal thoughts vanished, the BDD lessened, and my health improved. This break granted me the ability to embrace and plan for the New Year. I looked forward to further healing, becoming a grandmother, and even a wife. With Christina transitioning into motherhood in July, Stephine turning twenty-one in December, I would be on my way to fulfilling my mission, my hearts desire, to the best of my ability. On the contrary, I still battled with a debilitating mindset and longed to keep safe, knowing my daughters would need me in the future. I thought by settling down with Dave I would have a better chance of survival. However, this was not happening unless we wedded. I refused to live in sin and condemnation again. Before making such a commitment to relocate, I informed Dave of my need to remain in Connecticut for the remainder of the year. It was imperative I be present for the birth of my grandson, aid Christina during the first several months of motherhood, and celebrate Stephine's twenty-first birthday with her. Dave understood and accepted my heart's desires.

After careful consideration, Dave and I decided to wed during our time in Florida. Due to my disorder, we decided on a private wedding. Over time, we had learned how to work around it—the simpler the better. In April, we exchanged wedding vows near our home in Florida. Thank goodness, the BDD did not accompany us. It remained dormant, which granted us the freedom to enjoy our remaining time together before I headed back to Connecticut at the end of May.

While away, a great deal of change unfolded at my place of employment. My boss sent me an email stating that several employees left. He offered me the opportunity to work the morning shift when I returned. Without a doubt, there was no way possible I could return and work the evening shift I had previously held. Thankful, I accepted the new position. I counted it a blessing, an answer to my prayers.

As the end of May approached, with Christina's impending motherhood, Stephine scheduled for a tonsillectomy, and work waiting, Dave and I headed back. During the ride, I relished the thought of becoming a grandmother. I hoped to return in time for

Christina's baby shower. I also looked forward to reconnecting with Stephine, wanting to congratulate her for completing another semester at college. She studied to become a dental hygienist and the course load was tough. She deserved a huge pat on the back.

We survived our long, two-day trip, Dave stayed several days before flying back, and I pressed on, fulfilling my commitments to the Lord, my daughters and work. With my BDD in remission, I enjoyed Christina's baby shower. No props, no hats were required. The image in my mirror radiated something different. A more pleasant reflection stared back at me as my inner life continued to be cleansed. The time away aided me in relinquishing more wounds from my past as I worked on this book, a true lifesaver. I delighted in the baby shower without any evil spirit lurking within. I adored watching Christina unwrap gift after gift after gift. What made this occasion even more joyous was the fact that Stephine decided to attend. My daughters never had a good relationship and this breakthrough was a miracle for me to witness. Before settling down for the night, I fervently thanked God for preserving my life and allowing me to share in this milestone.

"Delight yourself in the LORD and he will give you the desires of your heart." —Psalm 37:4 (NIV)

Upon returning to work, I found I truly enjoyed working the morning shift. I did not have to deal with the unpleasant evening members and the new shift shielded me from the suicidal thoughts I had encountered during closing hours. Throughout the week, a group of women greeted me with hugs and congratulations. They had a beautiful card and a gracious wedding gift waiting. I never expected such generosity. It made me aware of what an awesome group of women God had placed in my life in spite of a handful of bad apples. Working the new shift, I formed fresh relationships with other members. I believed God rewarded me with a nicer crop of women because I remained pleasant to the ones who treated me rudely at night. I passed my test and He was pleased.

Mid-July approached and so did the arrival of my grandson, Michael. I never imagined I would witness so many blessed events. Aiding Christina through this awesome time of her life was so surreal. I looked forward to accompanying her to the hospital. While in labor, her contractions caused her a great deal of pain. Often I rubbed her back hoping to relieve some of her discomfort. As tears welled up in her eyes, so did mine. She ached and I bore her pain too. Scheduled for a C-section, they took her into the delivery room. The nurses wheeled her away and I prayed for her wellbeing and the baby. Shortly after, Mike, the baby's father came out with the biggest smile on his face and announced that both mom and baby were fine. I exhaled a huge sigh of relief when I heard the news.

Bliss filled my heart as I cuddled my grandson, Michael, for the very first time. The little critter swaddled in my arms amazed me, as his soft, delicate skin touched mine. I never imagined I would make it to grand-motherhood. I glanced over to Christina and suddenly viewed her differently. No longer did I see her as my little girl. She grew into a new position, the role of a mother. Our relationship shifted into a new realm. Yes, she will always be my daughter, but now we were both mothers too. Right away, I nicknamed him, Mickey G, short for Michael George.

Love, joy, and peace inundated me as I acknowledged more and more as to why God directed me back to Connecticut. Clearly, He had many reasons that I had no knowledge of—my water baptism, a deeper walk and dependence on Him, the birth of my grandson, and further closeness with my daughters.

Happiness filled me as I shared in the first several months of my grandson, Michael's life. Joy filled my core each time I held him in my arms. The aroma of his body brought back memories of when my daughters were little. Each time I visited, amazement filled my mind as I acknowledged Michael's growth. I adored all the charming outfits Christina dressed him in. As I guided and coached her during the first months of motherhood, our relationship deepened. We had endured many hardships over the years, but God blessed and restored our relationship.

As far as work, I recognized that while God widened my horizon in many areas, I remained limited at work with my BDD. I had faith that in His perfect timing he would remove the encumbrance. Regardless of my infirmity, I developed stronger friendships with many of the women. I loved sharing my faith with a select group of them. Our "God" talks were awesome—sermons in and of themselves. I knew in my heart that I could not keep my faith silent or hidden. I spoke openly anytime an opportunity presented itself. Many of the women knew about my writing. They cheered me on–especially with the children's Christmas book, excited and anxious to see it published.

Some issues at work brought discomfort. A few of the members hounded me about wearing a hat. Yet, their meddling did not disturb me as it had before. They had no clue of the battle I endured. Once my memoir was published, if they chose to read it, they would understand more fully. The other problem was my weekly requirement to go into public places and distribute promotional literature for my boss. It nearly destroyed me every time I went out to distribute the stuff. I never talked to my boss regarding my psychological illness and the fear of going out in public. I did not feel comfortable sharing this area of weakness with him. I knew I would return to Florida soon, so I toughed it out, no matter how anxious it made me. Dave, fully aware of my discomfort, could not wait for my employment to end. He feared I would end up in the hospital again. Yet, he knew how badly I desired to stay employed. Dave was the "wind beneath my wings." He supported my need for independence, rather than enabling me. I could have easily remained captive, housebound, never pressing through my fears and challenges had he sent me money.

Excited, Stephine's twenty-first birthday arrived. Stephine, Rob, and I went to a well-known pizza restaurant to celebrate. We had a wonderful time while we ate, chatted, and reminisced. Thank goodness, the BDD did not trouble me. As mentioned above, God widened my borders in areas that meant the most to me and my loved ones, yet still kept limitations on others. Stephine, enjoyed dinner with us but was anxious to return home so she could go out and celebrate with her friends. I prayed that God would keep a protective hand on her as she advanced into adulthood.

A few weeks later my husband Dave, flew to Connecticut. He wanted to spend Christmas with us and help with my move to Florida. We invited everyone over on Christmas Eve for dinner. Dave and I cooked a scrupulous meal before they arrived. Overflowing with joy, I sorted through the gifts and piled them into individual bundles for my loved ones—Stephine, Christina, Mickey G, and his dad, Mike. I never imagined the day would unfold as splendidly as it did. I realized how far I had come in overcoming so many obstacles to my happiness.

Stephine arrived earlier than Christina and what a blessed encounter we shared. She was curious as to what I was working on when she arrived, "Merry Christmas Mom. What's that you're working on?"

"It's the manuscript to the children's Christmas book I've written. I just finished the drawings a little while ago."

"Oh that's nice. Do you have time to read it to me?" she asked, plopping on my bed.

Surprised, because she never had shown interest in my writing, I replied, "Sure, I'd love to read it to you."

I rested by her side and began reading the Christmas story to her. My heart pounded as I read it aloud. During this time, I believed God handed me a precious gift. I missed out in doing this kind of stuff with her when she was young. Now, many years later, He gave back those lost, stolen years. Finished, Stephine commented, "That's a cute story. Are you going to have it published for next Christmas?"

"I'm looking into having it published once I'm in Florida. I would love to see it completed by next Christmas."

Little did she know, all the time I worked on the Christmas book I prayed to God to use it in a special way. I hoped to share the true meaning of Christmas in a simple, childlike fashion, particularly with Stephine. She held no knowledge of its significance. It had bothered me that she was twenty-one now and never once stepped into a church—no weddings, no funerals, not even a Sunday service with me. However, God made that evening special by blessing me with the opportunity to share my Christmas story about Jesus with her.

Dave returned from the store, and Christina, Mike, and Mickey G, arrived. We had a grand time celebrating together. Everyone enjoyed the array of food and plentiful gifts. I held Mickey G, in my arms nearly all night, longing to keep him close to me. Christina dressed him in an adorable Santa suit with matching hat. Christina and Stephine brought gifts, but they were unnecessary. They themselves were my precious gifts. As usual, I acknowledged and thanked God for the enjoyment He bestowed upon us.

Christmas day arrived. I longed to make it to church regardless of the terrible weather. No way was a winter storm or the BDD going to keep me from attending. Excited, I placed my little black hat on and headed out the door. Dave, already outside cleaning and warming up the car, knew how important this outing was to me, being the last time I'd attend service at my church before heading to Florida. During service, I poured out my heart of gratitude as we celebrated the birth of Christ Jesus. I sat in awe throughout the entire service.

A few days later, Dave and I packed the car and once again headed to Florida. Sadness filled my heart when I placed my apartment keys on the counter for my landlord. A lot took place during the one and a half years I spent in that little apartment. Yet the best memories were stored in my heart along with the vast amount of pictures I had captured of my precious ones.

Christina and Stephine admitted they were going to miss me, but I assured them it was not the end. We would keep in touch, and I already had plans to return in July for Mickey G's first birthday. I wished farewell to the women at work. I never imagined I would grow close to others. I did not think I had it in me, but God proved me wrong as He continued to change me from within. Many of the members did not want me to leave. Yet I knew it was time–time for me to be with my husband, Dave. We longed to start the New Year off together.

"Therefore, if anyone is in Christ, he is a new creation; the old has gone, the new has come!" — 2 Corinthians 5:17 (NIV)

Dear God, for over forty years You and I traveled together through so many things. You were with me through the desert places of my existence, in the wake of all my suffering, sin, and rebellion, and for some reason You never gave up on me. Thank You for blessing me in so many ways and for granting me the desires of my heart. Lord, I am so thankful that Your Light shone into the darkest crevices of my heart, mind, and soul, You, saved me! Holy Spirit, I pray that You continuously transform me from the inside out, so that I can become more like Jesus. In Jesus' name I pray, Amen

- Do you realize that as you delight yourself in the Lord, He will give you the desires of your heart? What are those desires?
- What are some of your most precious "moments" you have spent with loved ones?
- Have you ever thought of writing a book about your life story?

"I'm thanking you, God, from a full heart, I'm writing the book on your wonders."

—Psalm 9:1 (TM)

Twenty-four

The Rise, Fall & Triumph

The first few weeks settling in brought heartache. I longed for my daughters, grandson, church, and even friends from work. Grief struck my heart. I loved them dearly, we had grown close, and now they were missing. I knew I would experience change, but I did not expect it to strike me as deeply as it did. I realized I was going through a grieving process and little by little, the grief peeled away. I acknowledged my loved ones were not gone forever, they just lived in another state, and I still played a vital role in their lives regardless of the distance between us. Often, Christina, Stephine, and I phoned one another, keeping in touch. Regularly, Christina emailed me updated pictures of Mickey G, which always brightened my day. Knowing we would be seeing each other in July gave us something to look forward to. On top of relocating, I experienced the "empty nest" syndrome. I had to find my new role, my new identity in order to keep living with purpose.

Now my life was focused on only Dave, myself, and of course the lingering BDD. I refused to allow the latter to get the best of me. I knew God still had plans to use me and no way could I allow my "hair" to thwart his will. According to scripture, He knew how many hairs were on my head, especially now with so few. Apparently, the vast amount of stress my body habitually suffered caused my hair to fall out excessively. The unpleasing sight in my mirror was no longer just a figment of my imagination, a BDD distortion. It was real! So real, I sought help to aid me through this unexpected episode. I refused to let my exposed scalp, the shedding of my hair, keep me housebound. I had too many important things to accomplish: finding a new church, publishing the Christmas book, and working on this book as well. I believed God knew where my heart was headed. I longed to fulfill my mission and desired to look and feel my best doing it.

I informed Dave of my concern and plausible need of getting a wig as my hair continued to thin, causing my disorder to rise again. He knew my struggle with going out in public and my longing to tend to the things I wanted to achieve outside of our home. We found a specialty shop that sold wigs. It was nice knowing that the owner understood my concern. Together we took nearly an hour to find the appropriate wig for my petite head. It took almost another hour for her to perform her miraculous works, cutting and trimming it to accommodate my features. We chatted while she hacked away at the wig resting on my head. She mentioned she did not dare go out in public without hers. She wanted to look her best for self-esteem, her husband, and church too.

With my back to the mirror, I had no idea what was taking place. She assured me I would be very pleased. She had many years experience doing what she loved the most. Once done, she turned me around and I could not believe my eyes. A huge smile adorned my face, accompanied by a sparkle in my eye. *Wow! What a difference. I love it!* I knew I would be on my way to embracing the things I sought to accomplish without hindrance. I recognized she held a gift, a divine knack to aid and comfort those undergoing change and acceptance of their appearance. Upon leaving, I thanked God for placing one of His working angels in my path. I believed He fated her to be a blessing unto others as she was to me. I hoped she fully recognized her awesome gift, her contribution to this imperfect world. The wig assisted me for a season, paving a way for me to press on.

With the advent of yet another New Year, I set goals and ambitions to accomplish the things I truly believed God wanted me to carry out. At this time, I knew employment was not an imperative issue. Previously, it produced a vast amount of distress on my body, mind, and soul. Now was the time for me to rest from that tribulation. Settled under one roof with my husband, Dave made this possible. Before, I had no choice but to work in order to live independently. The effort caused a great deal of distress on my weary soul. The Body Dysmorphic Disorder that nearly killed me was turning. I refused to battle with it and employment at this moment in my life. I had better things to tend to, instead of fighting against them. I settled down to work from home on my writing. I believed writing would aid in further healing. Thus, I pressed on in faith, hoping to fulfill the new desires in my heart.

First, I needed to find a church. Fortunately, during one of my flights to Florida, I sat near a young lad, traveling by himself, who was troubled over the turbulence we encountered. I did my best to comfort him through his distress. I told him I imagined God's finger positioned underneath the belly of the plane and He was not going to let anything bad happen to us. Listening, the frightened young boy calmed down and we chatted during the remainder of our flight. He suggested that I look into the church his grandparents attended and often brought him to. It just so happened to be located near my home. I decided to visit the church he recommended and right away felt at ease.

Each Sunday morning as I prepared for church, I donned my wig. I was not going to let that old, dreadful BDD get in my way. It was imperative for my survival to keep going forward. It paid off! I ended up becoming a member within a few months. The first and foremost goal I had set for the New Year and I had mastered it!

Not only did I succeed at finding a church, I pressed on with the publication of my Christmas book, hoping to have it published before the holidays. The desires of my heart could only come forth if I gave them the attention they required, regardless of my apprehension of going out in public. Fortunately, I found a wonderful writers' group close to home. The group and its leader, a local editor, assisted with editing and revisions. They had given me a lead to a local publishing company too. I followed the recommendation and by the end of January signed a contract with them to publish my children's Christmas picture book. From this point, I marveled in the hope of seeing my "baby", my first book come to life, and be released by the end of May. *I hope it's done before my trip to Connecticut in July. I cannot wait to share it with Christina and Stephine. I would love to have a Christmas in July book signing at Curves.*

With this dream in the hands of the publishing company, illustrator, and graphic designer, I pressed on to my newest goal—finishing this book. It was time to begin the demanding process of finishing the few chapters that remained and then editing and revisions. Writing each chapter was one thing, having to re-examine and rewrite was a relentless journey in and of itself. It meant going back to chapter one in order to begin this tedious process. This also involved recapturing the grueling episodes, marveling in the good ones, and recognizing my continuous journey towards God.

Months flew by while I engaged in my new goals. Then one day, my doorbell rang, our UPS driver delivered a package. Exhilaration twirled around me, already knowing what he was delivering. "They're here! They're here!" I shouted to Dave. "My baby is here!"

Dave could not open the package fast enough for me to grab hold of one of them. It was the children's picture book, *The True Meaning of Christmas, The Greatest Gift of All*, in its completion. Holding it in my hands, Dave and I marveled over it. Jubilation bubbled in my heart as I settled into my black leather office chair with a cup of tea to read the beautifully illustrated book. Tears of happiness cascaded down my face as I delighted in the vision of my daughter Christina reading it to Mickey G in years to come. For over two years, I hoped and prayed that this awe-inspiring dream would come true and it finally had. I believed in my heart that it would leave an impression on society, even if I did not witness it in my time here on earth. If only one child, just one, understands the true meaning of Christmas because of my book, it will be a success.

As weeks passed, I struggled using the wig I purchased. For six months, it had served me well. It granted me rest from my distressing grooming ritual, bringing me a temporary reprieve. Without the constant war in the mirror, God's love took up residence more and more, creating the healing I so desperately needed. However, now a subtle prompting in my heart coerced me to think it was time— time to put my wig away and go forward without it. Fear surrounded me at this crossroad of letting go of my trusty resource. Mind you, for six months, my wig accompanied me wherever I went. We attended church together, ventured out biweekly to participate in the writers group, and nearly everywhere else we roamed. The majority of people I encountered never saw me without it on–most were unaware I even wore a wig. More frightening, I did not know what I would encounter in the mirror. Would the gruesome image reappear? Would my body, soul, and mind go back to the dilapidated state it once held? What would people say or think of my real look? Obviously, they would notice the huge change, the wig was long and full, and my hair was extremely short and thin. Thus, I grappled for several weeks with the decision of going wigless, into the public eye.

With my trip to Connecticut approaching for Mickey G's first birthday, and a scheduled book signing of the Christmas book, I wrestled with the wig dilemma more and more. *Should I take it? Should I leave it? Will my BDD get in my way of enjoying these cherished times.* The first book event was at my editor, Dona Lee's shop. My wig and I attended the special occasion, a pleasant time we had as people wandered about yet I felt a tad of apprehension that evening. It seemed like everyone else walked around comfortable in his or her own skin except for me. I hid behind a wig that I now wanted to dispose of, so the real me could emerge. I started to crave this unfolding, this opening, more and more as my flight day approached. Sure enough, the night before my trip I made a clear-cut decision not to wear or even pack the wig. I felt strong enough in my faith. I did not need it any longer and my trip would turn out just fine. God performed marvelous things within me and it was time to step out into society without the use of my companion, my wig. I chose to go forward with God instead. I trusted in Him to keep the all-consuming ugly images in my mirror at bay.

Morning came and also the time to groom and head to the airport. Thank goodness, no war broke out as I prepared for the day. Dave kept a distance—he stayed far, far away from our bathroom, giving me time to get ready. Besides, he was not sure if he would encounter the old me or the improved me. When done, I politely told him, "Honey I'm ready. I did great in the bathroom. I'm so glad I decided not to fuss with the wig." Dave, at ease, chauffeured me to the airport. Pure delight wrapped itself around me as I acknowledged God's kindness. I rested in great assurance that my trip would be better without the wig. I had left it behind! I surrendered to the nudging in my heart and stepped out in faith knowing I no longer needed my crutch.

"Your beauty should not come from outward adornment, such as braided hair and the wearing of gold jewelry or fine clothes. Instead, it should be that of your inner self, the unfading beauty of a gentle and quiet spirit, which is of great worth in God's sight."
—1 Peter 3:3-4 (NIV)

Bliss filled my heart when I arrived in Connecticut, a pure delight to walk in freedom. The refining and cultivating process God had me in showed as I marched to the sound of a different drum. I returned to the delightful melody of a merry-go-around instead of riding the untamed roller coaster I so often rode in the past. I could not wait to see Stephine, Christina, and Mickey G. It had been nearly seven months. Once in my rental car, I immediately phoned both girls.

Christina looked forward to my visit after I spent time with Stephine first.

Stephine and I enjoyed our time together. We shopped for hours, looking at clothes for her upcoming vacation to California with her dad. We had a blast! We lost sight of time. Christina phoned, anxious to find out when I would be heading to her place. I assured her I was fine and I would be there as soon as Stephine and I checked out.

I was blown away when I saw my grandson Mickey G. He had grown so much. At first, he cried, as I was a stranger to him. However, as time passed he warmed up. I was pleased to see how devoted Christina was in her role as a mother. We enjoyed planning for the upcoming party. I could not believe Mickey G was turning one already. My trip transitioned from one blessing to the next without any flare-ups in the mirror. Thank God, my disorder remained dormant during these priceless moments.

I scheduled my book signing Saturday morning at *Curves*, my previous place of employment. Immediately afterward, I planned to attend Mickey G's, birthday party. This agenda was unheard of not too long ago–attending not just one, but two back-to-back events had been beyond my reach. Yet with God's help and my determination to overcome, I surpassed my old, unsupportive mindset. Once again, He widened my borders, and even removed the "thorn in my flesh" during this breathtaking trip.

The book signing turned out great. A bouquet of flowers awaited me along with balloons and a congratulation banner. Jess and Pat, previous coworkers, offered a generous tray of Christmas cookies and fresh fruit. We had a wonderful time delighting in the celebration of my first book. Our reunion was refreshing. The best thing—I did not wear a hat! Many of them never saw me without one and to them this was a big surprise in and of itself. As I waved goodbye to the women, I felt as though I was on cloud nine and the day and fun had just begun.

With the sold-out book signing over, I set out to embrace the second part of the day—Mickey G's first birthday. To experience life without fear, no anxiety, or masks continued to awe me. I wanted to pinch myself to make sure I was not dreaming. Joy, peace, and happiness flooded me all day long. Watching Christina help Mickey G open his gifts brought back memories of her first birthday. Now twenty-five years later, I witnessed her celebrating her precious son's first birthday. After all the gifts were unwrapped, she placed his tiny customized *Blues Clues* cake in front of him. Seated in his highchair he devoured it. Apparently, it was his first time having a sugary sweet and it showed as he rocked back and forth endlessly. We laughed over the blue icing smeared on his face, head, and body. We had a marvelous time. Truly, I did not want the day to end. As night fell, I thanked God for the full day of celebration and joy.

I attended church the following day. There was no way I would miss going. I sought to give thanks and appreciation to God. I also wanted to say hello to Bishop J and give him a surprise gift. Service ended and I patiently waited in line to greet him. I must have been radiating like a beacon of light when he saw me. He immediately noted how illuminated I looked. I believe it was due to the great deal of time I spent with God. The Light of the Holy Spirit transcended from me, darkness no longer reigned in my soul. Like a little girl bringing her daddy a gift, I humbly handed Bishop J a copy of my Christmas book. It put a smile on his face. As we talked, I professed all the wonderful things God was doing in my life. I explained how it seemed as though I had finally entered into the Promised Land; God had shown me the way out of the forbidding wilderness. Bishop J delighted in my upturn and conquest.

So many monumental and priceless moments took place during this ten-day excursion. However, as my departure date approached, I looked forward to returning home to my husband, Dave. As wonderful as the trip was, I missed him. Besides, during the last few days, excruciating pain pierced the back of my neck, making it nearly impossible to drive. *God please heal this pain before I have to drive to the airport.* Thank goodness, I found comfort, the morning of my departure. The awful pain dissipated, God answered my prayer.

Finally home, the following day, my inner being collapsed. My pleasant carousel ride stopped, tossing me back on the death-defying roller coaster. Upon awakening, trepidation filled me. As it was Sunday, I desired to go to church, yet struggled with choosing to wear my wig or not. I had done great in Connecticut without it, now it was time for me to embrace going wigless here. I accepted my looks in the company of my loved ones, now I had to do the same here. I feared their speculation and possible rejection. Paralyzed by fear and the notion of having an evil BDD attack, I surrendered. I put my wig on and went to church. For the first time ever, I did not enjoy service. I felt miserable leaving the enhanced, real me behind, while I dragged the old dejected me to church. When service ended, I rushed home and tore the wig off. I did not desire to wear it anymore. It served its purpose for a season and now I longed to find contentment in my God-given attire. Thus, I determined not to wrestle with it any longer.

Unfortunately, the dilemma did not stop without any problems. The following day, suicidal thoughts unexpectedly rushed through my mind. I had not encountered this evil in a long time—well over a year—an all time record for me. A tremendous wave of despair overwhelmed me. I envisioned the rope I needed to knot to end my pain forever. I could not handle the sudden white to black situation. *Did Satan invade my thoughts overnight? Did the high altitude from the plane mess my equilibrium? Oh no! Am I in another spiritual battle?* Whatever the culprit was, it sought to obstruct me from the progressive path I had journeyed, as thoughts of suicide steadily infiltrated my mind. I hid this desolation from Dave as I struggled to press on with my writing.

With no reprieve from my despair, another day of suicidal visions swamped me. Exhausted and fatigued by my inner misery, I decided to take an evening walk with Dave. I hoped it would ease some of my anxiety. Dave was not aware that thoughts of death prowled once again inside my head. Shortly after our walk, I experienced a sharp pain in my neck and jaw. Within minutes, it intensified and traveled down my arms. As the pain worsened, I told Dave something was wrong. I did not feel well, and headed to the bedroom to lay down. Upon resting on the bed, the excruciating pain penetrated my chest cavity. Each time I tried to breathe, it felt as if someone had my muscles in a vise, cranking them tighter and tighter. With the pain out of control, I yelled to Dave in unreserved anguish. "Something is wrong. The pain is horrible. You might have to take me to the hospital if it gets worse." Within seconds, my face grew clammy and moist. I sweated profusely as the pain pulsated through my entire upper body, doubling in intensity. At this point, Dave and I knew it was time to rush me to the hospital.

During the ride, I tried not to breathe; each stabbing breath offered only additional suffering. Dave, uncertain of what was happening, drove directly to the emergency entrance. Upon entering, he told the nurses I was experiencing chest pains. They rushed me in, skipping past the vast crowd of people in the waiting room. Right away, they gave me aspirin, took a chest x-ray, and drew blood.

They thought I was having a heart attack. I was mystified. Just an hour prior, I harbored thoughts of suicide. Now I lay in wait wondering if I was going to die without my doing. The alarming, somewhat uncanny event stopped my suicidal inclinations. To alleviate the excruciating pain they administered morphine as we waited for the test results. For hours, I laid in the hospital bed, with pain pulsating through my chest and arms in spite of the morphine. The test results confirmed it was a heart attack. When the doctor informed me of such, I grew numb in disbelief.

Dave and I were dumbfounded by the news. We never imagined a woman my age—forty-four, active, with a healthy eating regimen—would encounter such a thing. The emergency room physician informed me I would be staying a day or two for further testing and observation. Five hours later the pain eased and they wheeled me into a private room, accompanied by an array of monitoring devises. As time passed, I absorbed the shocking news, and acknowledged that God was not finished with me yet.

The following day the heart surgeon arrived. He advised I needed exploratory surgery so he could determine the severity of the heart attack. Sure enough, he found the blockage, but due to the location and size of the vessel, he felt it would be best to leave it alone. He ordered me to stay an extra day to recover from the surgery and to monitor my damaged heart. My family was shocked by the news. They all thought I would be the last one to have a heart attack. Christina and Stephine were glad to hear I was ok. They too were startled.

Released from the hospital, the first few weeks of recovery nearly killed me. Unable to exercise drove me insane; a vital part of my daily existence was taken away. I didn't have the strength to even walk down the driveway. Regardless, I followed my doctor's recommendations and walked a little bit further each day. Dave accompanied me every step of the way, wanting to make sure I was ok. Many times, out of breath and exhausted, I turned around and went back home. Discouraged, I had never expected to experience such limitations.

"My flesh and my heart may fail, but God is the strength of my heart and my portion forever. But as for me it is good to be near God. I have made the Sovereign Lord my refuge; I will tell of all your deeds."
—Psalm 73:26, 28 (NIV)

I sought to make good use of my recovery time and continued to work on this book. As time evolved, I longed to return to church. As my desire increased, suicidal thoughts surfaced once again. I still feared going out in public. For nearly thirty excruciating days I cried, screamed, and spoke dreadful things to Dave about myself. "I hate my looks. I cannot live in this ugly body. I'd rather be dead than be trapped inside this body." He comforted and consoled me through out this horrifying nightmare. Daily, he listened and encouraged me through this valley of darkness. I felt even more miserable dumping my inner misery on him, which intensified my thoughts of suicide. I tumbled into a black abyss, again.

Nearing my forty-fifth birthday, I dreaded it. I didn't want to face another day, let alone another year. Through this entire uproar, I read my Bible, prayed to God, and tuned in to sermons. However, the dreadful stronghold of suicide would not flee. A few flickering moments of hope entered my mind and heart offering a brief view of sanity. Yet each time I grasped the little beam of light, forces of darkness blanketed me. At my weakest point, two days before my birthday, while showering the suicidal thoughts besieged me. *Dave is not here. This is the perfect time for me to hang myself. I cannot keep living like this!*

At this pivotal moment, I panicked over the thought of actually acting on my deadly emotions. All the other times I tried to commit suicide I was under the influence of either medication, alcohol, or both. This time I was not under the influence of anything, other than the evil spirit currently invading my mind. I had not had a drink or used any medications since my last attempt, nearly three years prior. Out of dire distress, I dropped to the shower floor and prayed for help. *God break this oppression. God give me a life worth living. God rescue me from this terror.* I kept chanting this appeal repeatedly as water cascaded down my trembling fetal position. The shower water grew cooler and cooler as I continued to rock my hunched over body endlessly. It took every once of energy to rise from the shower floor as I released my last cries of mercy and anguish.

"The Lord will rescue me from every evil attack and will bring me safely to his heavenly kingdom. To him be glory for ever and ever. Amen." —2 Timothy 4:18 (NIV)

Miraculously, when I opened the shower door God's peace filled me. My oppression broke. The evil force that nearly killed me fled down my shower drain along with my tears of sorrow. In my heart, I knew God broke the generational curse of suicide handed down to me. The shackles of doom that once bound me came undone, freeing me from the enemy camp. My death sentence ended. God resuscitated me back to life. Hope, peace, and great assurance stirred within my heart, granting me the ability to grasp hold of the life God offered. He stepped down low and rescued me from the vile abyss that desired to kill me. Had I not dropped to my knees and cried out to God when I did, I do not believe you would be reading about the triumph now.

Dave witnessed my sudden upturn in Spirit, behavior, and speech, "Honey, I'm so glad to have my wife back. I'm happy that you're feeling better."

Two days later, Dave and I went out to celebrate my forty-fifth birthday. I embraced it filled with joy and peace. I desired no gifts. I believe God gave me all I needed, the stamina and courage to carry on with living. That same weekend, I attended church with no wig. I made it through my grooming ritual fine. I felt at ease and confident. Not only did I master attending church wigless, I visited my editor's gallery as well. I had not seen her all summer long due to the heart attack. Immediately we hugged. I missed her a lot, and looked forward to returning to our writing sessions. Truly, God reopened doors of opportunities along with freedom from the use of a wig and the BDD.

At the same time my revival took place, Dave and I participated in a 5k suicide awareness and prevention walk. I sought to participate in remembrance of my father's death, forty years prior, my sister, Kim's death, three years prior, and to celebrate my survival after five attempts. As bizarre as this may seem, I planned to take part in this event even before my latest chilling entanglement with the overpowering thoughts of suicide. I had imagined attending this event would aid in my healing. In my heart, I felt my participation would close the door to any further attempts. I sought to incorporate the "Walk for Life" event into the final chapter of this book. It was imperative for me to bring everything dark into the light in order to escape my adversary. As you can see, I brought to light many, many issues in order to be set free from them.

During the 5K event, I cried as I witnessed so many other people hurting over the loss of their loved ones. As I stood among the hundreds of attendees, I wept even more as I thought about the possibility of one of my daughters attending such an event in remembrance of me. *Thank God, I'm alive. I wouldn't want to be the reason for one of them to attend an event like this.* I vowed I would never put either one of my girls in this position. Toward the end, everyone who lost a loved one was handed a pink envelope with a live butterfly tucked within. Others attending were given colorful bottles of bubbles. On the count of three, we were instructed to release our butterflies into the air in remembrance of our loved ones, while the others blew bubbles. Within seconds, dozens and dozens of butterflies flew around among the vast amounts of bubbles floating in the air. It seemed like a fantasyland as the butterflies and bubbles twirled all around me. As I glanced to the sky, I acknowledged my beloved ones and thanked God that I was still here. Thank goodness, Dave had a hanky. By the time the event ended, it was soaked due to my continuous tears of joy and thankfulness. Leaving, I felt blessed to have had the opportunity to attend. It marked a new beginning of life for me, one that did not include suicide. Lord willing, I will participate again and be a source of help to those touched by this heartbreaking matter.

One day, out of the clear blue sky, I realized my BDD had disappeared. After showering, I groomed and finished within a smidgeon of a time. Uncontrollably, I laughed and chuckled thinking where did my BDD go. Dave heard me laughing hysterically and asked, "What's so funny?"

I replied, while still overly amused, "I lost my BDD, I can't find it. Do you know where it is? Did you take it from me? I don't know what I'm going to do without it."

"I'm so glad you're doing so well. It's nice to see you happy," Dave noted.

"I can't wait to finish the last chapter of my book. It has been one heck of a mission. I hope and pray it helps at least one other person."

"I'm sure it's going to help a lot of people. It's one unbelievable story," Dave commented.

"Yea! I am glad I survived it. I cannot wait to see what God has in store for me next. My newest heart's desire is to be an inspirational speaker, a beacon of "Light" to those sitting in darkness with wounded, broken hearts."

"God made my life complete when I placed all the pieces before him. When I got my act together, he gave me a fresh start. Now I'm alert to God's ways; I don't take God for granted. Every day I review the ways he works; I try not to miss a trick. I feel put back together, and I'm watching my step. God rewrote the text of my life when I opened the book of my heart to his eyes."

—Psalm 18:20-24 (TM)

Father God, I pray on behalf of all who read this book. I pray that You would do a marvelous thing within each one of their lives. I ask in faith that You would tug on the hearts of those that do not yet have a relationship with You. I hope that they will seek to invite Your Son, Jesus, into their hearts and lives, making Him their Lord and Savior. I ask that You would send a ministry of healing into the lives of those who have been wounded by the calamities and chaos of this world. All who are in dire need of Your mercy, grace, and unconditional love. May You turn their sorrow into joy. I ask that You do a new thing in each one of their lives as they seek You with all their hearts, souls, and minds. Father God, I petition that You fill each receptive heart with Your Spirit. I ask that You call forth Your beloved daughters out of darkness and into the glorious Light of Your Son and kingdom purposes. Loosen them from the chains of their past and set them free to journey on the narrow, chosen path You destined for them. In Jesus' name I pray, Amen

- Do you realize that God loves you no matter what has taken place in your life, how many mistakes you have made, and regardless of where you might be right now?
- Are you ready to open the book of your heart to Him…so He can help you rewrite the text of your life?
- Cry out to God! Invite His Holy Spirit into your painful circumstances and ask the Lord to walk with you through whatever issue(s) you need to face. Surely, He will lead you in triumphant to the "Light" at the end of your dark tunnel.

P.S. Do not forget to read the ***"Arise My Daughter"*** message provided on the following pages. It is a blessed Word written and intended for you.

Let your arising new journey with the Lord begin…

Arise My Daughter

"Arise, shine, for your light has come, and the glory of the Lord rises upon you." —Isaiah 60:1 (NIV)

My beloved daughter, it is time for you to arise and take your stance in the Light of My Son. I, your heavenly Father, am calling you out of darkness. Arise from your affliction for My power within you is greater than your despondency. Healing, restoration, and freedom await, but you must have faith. I beckon you to arise to the new things I seek to do within, for, and through you.

Clearly, you do not perceive that your prison sentence, inner turmoil, and suffering, is over. I, the Lord, have removed the chains that bind you. Your shackles are loose, and your prison doors are open. In your darkness, I heard your weeping and now I offer you My peace. Freedom and new life awaits but you must choose to come out of captivity. My precious daughter, it is time for you to behold, step forward, and partake in the new things I set before you.

Stop mulling over old wounds, hurts, and grudges. Abandon victimization, self-pity, and the lies of the enemy. He has stolen from you long enough. I will not tolerate it any longer! You are My child, a daughter of the King. I want you to fight and recapture that which the enemy has stolen. Reclaim your life, family, joy, and peace. Reclaim your freedom to live for Me, the One who is bringing you out of darkness and into the Light.

It is time for you to acknowledge you are well, strong, and capable of moving on. With your head held high, step forward into the higher ground I bequeath unto you. Abstain from relying on others, fully lean and trust in Me. I have wonderful plans to use you in unimaginable ways, if you are willing to abandon your poverty-ridden condition. You are an heir to the King of kings. I seek to robe you with a garment of honor and virtue as you discard your tattered sackcloth. I seek to adorn you with a crown of beauty and joy as you arise from the ashes.

Awake! Your liberty bell is ringing. Do you not hear it? My Light is shining upon you. Do you not see it? My power is within you. Do you not sense it? The enemy has no claim on you any longer. My beloved Son, Jesus, paid a great price for your release. You are mine! Grab hold, claim, and embrace your new life and freedom in Christ. My Word says, "So if the Son sets you free, you will be free indeed." John 8:36 (NIV)

At times it may seem scary, but do not fear for I am with you. At times, you may seek to retreat to your old familiar grounds, but this is unwise. At times, you will have questions and even encounter doubt, but remember morning, noon, and night I am with you. Talk with me as we breathe, live, and work together. Let us walk closely together in the new journey, plan, and future I have prepared for you.

Arise My Daughter…step out in faith…abiding, leaning, and trusting in Me daily.

Love,

Your Heavenly Father

"For I know the plans I have for you," declares the Lord, "plans to prosper you and not to harm you, plans to give you hope and a future." —Jeremiah 29:11 (NIV)

Prayer for a Personal Relationship with the Lord

Father God,

I believe and confess with my mouth that Jesus Christ is Your Son, the Savior of the world. I believe He died on the cross for me and bore all my sins, paying the price for them. I believe in my heart that You raised Jesus from the dead. I ask You to forgive me of my sins. I confess Jesus as my Lord. According to Your Word, I am saved and will spend eternity with you! Help me to live a life that is pleasing to You. Amen

Name: _____

Date: _____

Supporting Scriptures:

᛫ "For God so loved the world that he gave his one and only Son, that whoever believes in him shall not perish but have eternal life." —John 3:16 (NIV)

᛫ "That if you confess with your mouth, "Jesus is Lord," and believe in your heart that God raised him from the dead, you will be saved. For it is with your heart that you believe and are justified, and it is with your mouth that you confess and are saved." —Romans 10:9-10 (NIV)

᛫ "And we have seen and testify that the Father has sent his Son to be the Savior of the world. If anyone acknowledges that Jesus is the Son of God, God lives in him and he in God." —1 John 4:14-15 (NIV)

Additional Resources

National Suicide Prevention Life Line

www.suicidepreventionlifeline.org

The BDD Foundation

www.thebddfoundation.com

National Alliance on Mental Illness

www.nami.org

International OCD Foundation

www.ocfoundation.org

www.ocfoundation.org/bdd

National Domestic Violence Hotline

www.thehotline.org

National Eating Disorder Foundation

www.nationaleatingdisorders.org

GriefShare

www.griefshare.org

Focus on the Family

www.focusonthefamily.com

Celebrate Recovery

www.celebraterecovery.com

Epilogue

Some may wonder whether my upturn in spirit lasted, if those appalling visions in my mirror returned, or if I ended up back on the "wild roller coaster." I will admit there were a few occasions when the BDD reared it's "ugly" head because of certain triggers; such as others trying to widen my borders, or me taking on to many things at once. Learning to live within the parameters of life that God has set for me is a vital key to staying on track. When God tells me to slow down or stay put, I listen and obey. When He widens my borders, presenting new opportunities to reach out and serve, I diligently seek to stay in step with His Spirit.

As my healing took root, I became a women's Christian devotional writer and Blog Mentor for a wonderful organization, *TruthMedia/PowertoChange*. To date, I have written over seventy inspiring devotionals that have been published and released to over 20,000 women worldwide. Here is the link to the devotional blog site: http://powertochange.com/blogposts/author/balpert/. It has been a blessing to minister to women all over the world from the comfort of my home. I'm also a contributing Author for *Chicken Soup for the Soul: Devotional Stories for Wives.* On top of that, God equipped me to become a small women's group leader. I delight in encouraging, edifying, and comforting women with Biblical truth.

My husband Dave and I are experiencing the best years of our married lives now. My daughters and grandson are doing well. My newest heart's desire is to compile a devotional journal, ***"Read, Pray & Journal your way through…"***

If this book has helped you, I would love to hear from you! Feel free to contact me at - **Arisemydaughter@aol.com**

May God's blessings be with you!

Sincerely,

Barbara Alpert

Additional Books

By: Barbara Alpert

Arise My Daughter Devotional Journal
Available on Amazon.com (ISBN - 13: 978-148491894 or ISBN-10: 1484981898) or by contacting author

Read, Pray & Journal your way through…inspiring devotionals for every situation, you may encounter (Forthcoming – 2014) *

*Perfect for women's small group studies and/or personal spiritual growth

Children's Books

By: Barbara Alpert

The True Meaning of Christmas - The Greatest Gift of All
Available on Amazon.com (ISB #978-1-936051-18-2) or by contacting author

The Tale of the Four Palm Trees (forthcoming – 2014)

Made in the USA
Charleston, SC
05 July 2013